Artificial Intelligence and Social Ethics

Neepa Shah

Artificial Intelligence and Social Ethics

Springer

Neepa Shah
Gujarat Vidyapith
Ahmedabad, Gujarat, India

ISBN 978-981-96-8817-3 ISBN 978-981-96-8818-0 (eBook)
https://doi.org/10.1007/978-981-96-8818-0

This Springer imprint is published by the registered company Springer Nature Singapore Pte Ltd.
The registered company address is: 152 Beach Road, #21-01/04 Gateway East, Singapore 189721, Singapore

Contents

List of Figures

List of Tables

Chapter 1
The Worldview on Automation

In the modern world of technological advancements, most of the industries are nowadays using a number of machines for achieving various production phases such as assembling, processing and packaging. Such machines can be classified into various categories, ranging from simple lathe machines to computerized machines. Computerized machines, popularly known as information and communications technology (ICT), were initially used for data handling but gradually they had been used to perform many cognitive tasks as well. People are using ICT on a daily basis to achieve multiple objectives, starting from daily transactions to taking decisions for future scope and trends with a view to sustain in this competitive world for their investment. Earlier, computerization had been used for faster execution and to maintain accuracy in data computation. However, along with computation, an advanced technology called Artificial Intelligence (AI) has entered the scenario in order to provide intelligent assistance to human beings, and proving its effectiveness in every aspect of life, has taken a lead role in ICT. Consequently, a new relationship changing various dimensions of the world has been established between human beings and machines.

The relationship between humans and machines is becoming more intense with time; daily human activities in most cases are almost impossible without the intervention of machines. In other words, reliance on such technologies has shackled us to such an extent that decision-making without them seems beyond our reach. Therefore, the discussion on this relationship is inevitable while talking about modern technology. Technologies have pushed the human community under the dictatorship of the digital world which is centralized and makes human being completely dependent on it. The core attribute of the digital world is 'data', and a person who possesses this data will have the power in future.

After the Renaissance among the Western countries, there was acceptance of three things: liberty, equality and fraternity. It has been a long time since a philosopher wanted to establish democracy and equality among citizens. In fact, we find many democratic countries in the world today but equality and fraternity, due to one or

N. Shah, *Artificial Intelligence and Social Ethics*,
https://doi.org/10.1007/978-981-96-8818-0_1

another reason, are still not achieved. If liberty and equality were established on the foundation of fraternity, it would be robust and effective as well. Unfortunately, fraternity is lacking due to the independence of individuals. But now it is the time to look back and to find what was incorrect during that era that persistently affected the present. As far as independence is concerned, industrialization and automation have played an important role in the living standards of citizens across the globe. With the introduction of AI in every sector of industries, changes appeared rapidly and a profound relationship between man and machine has come into picture. Number of automation-based applications in the industry that are being developed under the wings of AI insist on rethinking the terms of liberty, equality and fraternity. It is also about to rethink the term independence because this technology makes human beings dependent on it.

In this chapter, we will learn how this transition occurred, and control of human beings has been unknowingly transferred to someone else. We will also learn who these 'someone' are and how blindly we all are following them in the name of technology. We would also discuss how the race of technology may affect every aspect of human life and what could be the possible problems/outcomes of its usage on the surface in the near future.

Artificial Intelligence

AI is a science that makes machines smart enough to make decisions which are typically taken by people using human intelligence. In other words, AI is the branch of computer science which attempts to replicate or simulate human intelligence in machines. Along with logical reasoning, it mainly depends on various algorithms of mathematics or statistics, but being an interdisciplinary science, it learns from the environment with the help of Machine Learning (ML) and Deep Learning (DL) algorithms. We will discuss ML and DL later, but for now, let us see how AI is defined by researchers. During World War II, a English mathematician named Alan Turing changed history with a simple question: 'Can machines think?' His research paper entitled 'Computing Machinery and Intelligence' (Turing, 1950), and its subsequent Turing Test helped the machine designers to establish the foundation of Artificial Intelligence.

Stuart Russell and Peter Norvig, in their groundbreaking textbook named, *Artificial Intelligence: A Modern Approach*, study the question of intelligent agents in machines. Hence, AI can also be called as 'the study of agents that receive precepts from the environment and perform actions' (Russell and Norvig, 2010). According to them, AI explores four different approaches that define the field of AI:

- Thinking humanly
- Thinking rationally
- Acting humanly
- Acting rationally

The first two points majorly deal with thought processes and reasoning processes, while the remaining two deal with behaviour. Professor Patrick Winston, another AI researcher at MIT, defines AI as 'algorithms enabled by constraints, exposed by representations that support models targeted at loops that tie thinking, perception and action together' (Winston, 1992). John McCarthy, who has paved a path for human level AI, defined AI as: 'It is the science and engineering of making intelligent machines, especially intelligent computer programmes. It is related to the similar task of using computers to understand human intelligence, but AI does not have to confine itself to methods that are biologically observable' (McCarthy, 2007). While comparing human and computer intelligence, he wrote—'Arthur R. Jensen [Jen, 98], a leading researcher in human intelligence, suggests "as a heuristic hypothesis" that all normal humans have the same intellectual mechanisms and that differences in intelligence are related to "quantitative biochemical and physiological conditions". I see them as speed, short term memory, and the ability to form accurate and retrievable long term memories. Whether or not Jensen is right about human intelligence, the situation in AI today is the reverse. Computer programmes have plenty of speed and memory but their abilities correspond to the intellectual mechanisms that programme designers understand well enough to put in programmes. Some abilities that children normally do not develop till they are teenagers may be in, and some abilities possessed by two year olds are still out. The matter is further complicated by the fact that the cognitive sciences still have not succeeded in determining exactly what the human abilities are. Very likely the organization of the intellectual mechanisms for AI can usefully be different from that in people. Whenever people do better than computers on some task or computers use a lot of computation to do as well as people, this demonstrates that the programme designers lack understanding of the intellectual mechanisms required to do the task efficiently' (McCarthy, 2007). Given definitions implicitly says that AI is not limited to those methods which are biologically observable but there can be more analysis based on actions and reactions of human behaviours. Some abilities which are developed in a child cannot be retained by computers through programme using human intelligence and some abilities that are not developed till teenage can be developed through programming. Current stage of AI is dealing with the problems of human understanding by dividing it further into two sub-categories ML and DL.

Looking at all the aforementioned facts and statements, it can be inferred that AI, ML and DL have taken a leading role in the current era of automation. According to the researchers general definitions of these three terms are given as following:

AI, ML and DL

Artificial Intelligence (AI), in terms of automation, can be defined as:

Programming-based techniques and procedures deployed to automate tasks for which the application of human intelligence was previously required but now it is done with the help of software developed for specific purposes.
Machine Learning (ML) is:
The use of algorithms and advanced statistical models to improve performance of different tasks. It is an approach to programming that enables the development of even more capable AI applications.
Deep Learning (DL) can be considered as:
This is a subset of Machine Learning. It is a field that is based on learning and self-improving computer algorithms. Deep Learning works with artificial neural networks, which is designed to replicate how humans think and learn.

All the above mentioned terms are widely used while discussing ICT, along with other fields where automation is carried out by various domains like agriculture, health care, transportation, entertainment, energy, defense, etc.

History of Automation

Automation has a long and layered story that started more than a thousand years ago. In the current era, advancement in automation is mainly associated with the applications of AI technologies. Throughout history, automation has been represented as changes of requirements and sustained against new environments; it has hardly been identified as a balanced process between human and nature. Automated machines were carried out to increase the production speed, consistency and precision that cannot be possible through human workers. Using computers, power of such machines had been gradually magnified by inculcating multiple methods including electrical, hydraulic and mechanical. Therefore, many organizations moved towards automation because they wanted to sustain in this competitive environment. Besides, there were many valid reasons for migration of their industries into automated one. A few of them are discussed below:

To increase productivity of human workers: An automated manufacturing unit increases the productivity of human workers. For example, movement from one place to another with raw materials is replaced by conveyor belts. Undoubtedly, it reduces the efforts of the workers, and their efficiency can be used for other human-led tasks.

To reduce cost of the labour: Deploying machineries for various tasks have decreased the overall cost of production. A machine deployed by an organization may require an initial investment of a large amount, but this one-time cost is too low compared to human wages. Then onwards, the organization must bear only the maintenance cost. Thus, these machines can replace human workers forever, leading the organization to reduce the cost of labour drastically.

Safety: It is considered as one of the most obvious reasons for automation as human safety is always a prime concern for any industry; there are very rare chances of accidents because all the difficult tasks are performed by machines. So, the possibility of human injury or fatality ratio is highly reduced.

Along with these, many other reasons are also given for conversion of a plant to automation mode such as to improve quality of product, customization of the product according to demand, etc. It might be true for some products where measurements are precise and static, but making of some other products or a new product requires creative work which certainly is not an outcome of a machine. Many handmade products are popular and this will not be replaced by automation. One more reason why automation is preferred is that it reduces the elapsed time between order placed and delivered.

In the world of cut-throat competition, while considering the requirement of new produces and noval creative ideas, a question paused for those organizations which are going towards automation is—'Do these organizations have one such order of production?' And they will not rush for another order later on! Ultimately, this leads to capitalization (O'Sullivan, 2009). Such practices started long ago.

Industrial Era to Automation Era

In the 17th century, the invention of 'lathe' is credited as the first machine tool that led to the invention of all machine tools. In the 18th century, the industrial revolution was in full swing; textile industry, cotton industry, steel industry, and paper industry were powered by industrialization with the use of either steam or water. In the early 19th century, manufacturing activities rapidly increased by electricity and thus, automation has been changed with the arrival of accurate electrical timers. During World War II (1939–45), electric automation made a great deal with the advancement of industrial automation as the production of tanks, fighter airplanes, and warships were instruments to change the game at that time. A couple of decades later, in 1980, the idea of converting the automated manufacturing units into computerized unit first came in the mind of engineers that replaced the manufacturing shops with robots. Let us see the history with the timeline of automation through industrialization.

Timeline of Automation

Though automation started more than a thousand years ago, it is mainly based on AI technologies these days. If we peep into the history of the last few years, we will be able to observe how information technology has galloped in the current age. To understand the revolution in the automation era, it is important to study the timeline of events that played a major role in changing the environment of industries through automation in the world. Table 1.1 illustrates the timeline of automation, with and without use of AI.

Table 1.1 Timeline of automation, with and without use of AI

1820	1920	1960	1980	1990	2000	2010 till *today*
A car was introduced	Lathe and other manufacturing unit are replaced by electric automated devices	Innovation of a computer as a numeric computing machine	Innovation of Personal Computer by IBM	A term robot was introduced	First robot developed by MIT that can express emotions	Apple's Siri released
Prototype of Analytical Engine developed	Industrial automation of manufacturing units like car manufacturing that was taking 12 h had been reduced to 1 and half hour	Failed research on NLP delayed further development by 10 years	The term Virtual Reality was coined	Hypertext and hyperlink invented and used for WWW	Checkers is solved by a team of researchers at the University of Alberta	Business Process Automation (BPA) has become more refined
	During WW-II, fighter planes, warships, tanks, etc. had been manufactured	Remarkable innovation in the field of robotics	Japan realized the power of AI and started a project, Fifth Generation Computer System (FGCS) but failed due to some reasons	'Deep Blue' defeated Gary Kasparov in chess	AI comes with two dimensions Machine Learning (ML) and later on as Deep Learning (DL)	AI-based luxury products like Alexa, Siri launched in the market

(continued)

Table 1.1 (continued)

1820	1920	1960	1980	1990	2000	2010 till *today*
	1950, Alan Turing devised a way to measure 'intelligence' of machine		First national conference on AI—American Association of Artificial Intelligence was held	NASA deployed first robotic system on the planet Mars	Many research activities have been started on the basis of ML and DL. Example: Google developed an autonomous car	
	Introduced the term 'Artificial Intelligence'					Various chatbots and AI-based tool like ChatGPT released

Invention of Computer and Related Technology

In 1837, Charles Babbage started producing Analytical Engine, a prototype machine. This device was first named 'computer'. The world was introduced to the term 'robot' in early 1900, but in 1940, Isaac Asimov created a robot and presented three laws for robotics. In 1948, robots were used to find obstacles abounding on the surface by using sensors for lights and bumps. In 1950, Alan Turing devised a method with an intention to measure the 'intelligence' of machines, and to test their ability of thinking. With this milestone, AI came into existence before the researcher; to be specific; it was the beginning of robotics developments.

In 1956, Dartmouth University introduced a term 'Artificial Intelligence' with a view to encourage research in the area of robotics. However, it could not get success because of a negative Natural Language Processing (NLP) report. NLP is an automatic manipulation of natural language like speech and text using computer programmes. During those days, the given commands were needed to be understood by robots for correct execution. Considering these primitive requirements, NLP was developed in earlier days.

Professor Lighthill of Cambridge University, in his research paper, offered a pessimistic forecast for AI, stating that 'in no part of the field have discoveries made so far produced the major impact that was then promised' (Lighthill, 1973). This was the time when AI research stepped out of the limelight. Although remarkable innovation in the field of robotics already came out in 1966, Automatic Language Processing Advisory Committee (ALPAC) report by the US Government in the same year found that AI research of machine translation was hopeless and committee stated 'a clear promise of effecting early cost reductions, or substantially improving performance, or meeting an operational need'. Hence, both the reports had shown a deadly effect on the research of AI and the government had cut down funding in AI technologies (Smith, McGuire, Huang and Yang, 2006).

Initially, AI researchers expected that the outcome of AI research will make everything autonomous in the world if the field of AI would be nurtured well. According to them, most of the problems could be solved by implementing these technologies so they also tried different learning methods to develop a few entertainment applications using AI.

The following are a few of very well-known applications for their successful implementation:

'Deep Blue' was a powerful machine with a specialized hardware which got a victory over Gary Kasparov, a legendary chess player. The programme was based on brute force that makes selection of one of the moves from the possible number of moves from a particular position. Another programming method which was used for the same purpose was based on heuristic factors. However, it was not successful in the early stages as very little work was done using this method. But, using the principle of learning based on heuristic factors, many games like 'AlphaGo' were developed later. Besides, expert systems like DENDREL and MYCIN were also developed for chemical components and medicinal processes, respectively.

Another attempt was made by Japan after realizing the opportunities in the field of AI; they initiated a project called Fifth Generation Computer System (FGCS) which was aimed at creating next generation machines with multiple processors specializing in logic programming. This project commenced during 1980 to 1981. Unfortunately, the project resulted in a failure due to many reasons, but one of the most prominent reasons was the heuristic factor—how to teach a computer to think.

Industrial Development

When scientific research had been declined due to failure, countries like USA and Japan has stopped their funding to AI related projects but industries were still working on AI. There were some applications that are succeed because of automation of the real (manual) process. Those system were not only based on AI but with the help of mechanical and electronics devices automation is done in very successful manner. Here, system was partially supported by AI. Given are few successful development where AI is involved.

The world of automation came across many developments in the industrial segment that have been automated by various systems like Supervisory Control and Data Acquisition (SCADA) and Energy Management System (EMS) that can control data acquisition and manage over large geographical areas. Other systems control, monitor and manage different industrial processes that are distributed but operated as loosely coupled systems; such systems are known as Distributed Control System (DCS). Building Automation System (BAS) is used to control various activities of a building or a plant such as safety, fire, security and human activities. Similarly, other industrial systems used for automation and industrial control systems are called Instruments and Control System, Safety Systems, and Process Control Systems (Hayden, Assante, Conway, 2014). All these systems are automation systems.

Nowadays automation is mainly mapped with AI technologies; those systems are assisted by AI that has changed the scenario in industries and home appliances. Hence, industrial development using AI was intially very slow but it was continue even after the failure reports of US and Japan. Now it is in the full gear.

AI in Last Two Decades

Till date, a number of AI technologies have been executed for transforming everyday life of a common man, and many new disciplines like Machine Learning, Knowledge-based System, Deep Learning and Computer Vision have emerged from the AI technologies.

AI technologies are integrated with a variety of sectors; there are numerous examples where AI, with human-like capabilities, is making an impact in the world by its deployment to many sectors such as finance, national security, health care, transportation, justice, etc.

The highlights of such sectors are discussed here:

Finance

AI has been widely introduced into the stock exchanges where, in the earlier time, the decision-making process was done by humans with the data available in the database and personal portfolio. Now with the help of AI decision-making, computers match the investor's interests with micro scale so that individuals can perform financial businesses easily, smoothly and quickly. Today, AI has developed more advanced computing power; data storage of large volume is now easier because it can work with multiple storage locations with precise computing. AI can also assist in finding frauds and identifying abnormalities of the transactions. Along with this, it also provides great aid to banks and credit lenders for making smarter decisions. Because of these capabilities, AI is used for identifying and pinpointing trends and risk factors. Hence, it ensures better information for future term planning.

Security

AI technology is used to process massive data of individuals, to learn the pattern of human behaviour and to identify suspicious activities from the videos captured through surveillance systems. Unlike traditional war systems, AI also assists warfare control systems by making decisions quickly as warfare is a critical time where decisions are needed to be taken most quickly. Such systems are developed to map automatic decisions with a view to launch AI assisted autonomous weapons. This process which is made for fatal outcomes is known as hyperwar at this time. Apart from the hyperwars, AI assisted malware can challenge the most sophisticated signature-based cyber protections which is competent enough to destroy any cyber defense system. In last few years, it has been a trend to migrate applications on the Cloud-based system where the Internet is the backbone. AI assisted systems are capable of breaking any protection, data and security on the Internet. Hence, such systems are always vulnerable on Cloud. More about Cloud Computing is discussed in latter part of the chapter. AI has also been used to find out fraudulent financial transactions in very few milliseconds; in this way, banks are able to trace unauthorized transactions or mischief done via online banking.

Health Care

Now AI technologies are being used to cure diseases in health care sectors across the world; AI support is widely considered as preventive measures for identifying weak cells in many patients. For example, many Hollywood celebrities have gone through such a diagnosis and, on the basis of reports, they underwent some advanced surgeries. Such systems are developed using ML and DL. Recently, a German company has developed an application using DL that can detect lymph nodes in the human body through Computer Tomography (West and Allen, 2018). Similarly, AI has also been applied to prevent congestive heart failure and heart related illnesses using electrocardiograms and cardiac MRI images. Along with this, AI-assisted applications are used to detect lung cancer more accurately than humans. It can also classify skin lesions in the skin images. In the field of medical science, AI is also used to find indications of diabetic symptoms through retinopathy in eye images besides earlier diagnosis of some diseases like Alzheimer (Wade, 2019). Doctors are utilizing various techniques to detect mental fatigue from eye-tracking data while a person is watching video too.

Furthermore, AI assists the pharmaceutical industry to develop any drug faster than ever before; many incidents are noted where AI-assisted algorithms have facilitated the process of drug-making that generally takes a number of years and investment of hundreds of millions. Besides, it is capable of discovering which characteristics indicate positive responses in a patient during treatment. In other words, AI-assisted systems can provide the right plan for the treatment of the patient (Schmitt). ML and DL are very effective at hunting new pharmaceutical opportunities because precise treatment options can be provided on the basis of a patient's medical history, lifestyle genetic database and dynamically changing pathologist test.

Justice

Justice and law enforcement can be possible through AI technological aids; many video and CCTV surveillance systems use the AI-assisted devices to identify the whereabouts of an individual through facial images. This identification can be done in less than one minute. This identification research can be carried out even when a person is wearing a mask or helmet or is blocked by some obstacle while clicked by the camera. It can also be used to control or monitor traffic rule violations or crimes committed. In addition to that, AI technologies are also useful in forensic DNA testing too (Rigano, 2019).

Transportation and Logistics

AI technologies ensure improvement of supply chains with better scheduling and routing. In the near future, it would directly affect the marketing system as it can provide better match for supply with given demand, can anticipate consumers' product needs and can choose better services for consumers. With the help of AI-assisted devices, it has been easy to provide real-time route information to the travelers and shipments. The ratio of errors has been drastically reduced in supply-chain networks because automated warehouses make efficient resource management and assign workforce with value added activities. Machine Learning algorithms can extract predictive insight for capacity planning and logistics for critical decision-making.

Areas Where AI Made Its Influence the Most

AI technologies are being developed potentially with a view to provide benefits to society and economy. Undoubtedly, the use of AI is boosting productivity; however, at the same time, there is an emerging need for skilled manpower as demand because new services and new products have been emerging everyday. In this era of technology, AI has been successfully applied to various sectors like retail, manufacturing, entertainment, health care, finance, marketing, crowd sourcing, travel and transportation, social media, E-commerce, etc. only because of its potential to change the impact. The discussion above is just a bird's eye view of AI technologies in various sectors that carry various innovations that are taking place in the automated era. Here, we will discuss details of each sector with its latest development through detailed research.

Transportation

Transportation is one of the domains where reliability and safety are considered as critical factors, therefore, AI is used to accomplish such tasks productively. On one hand, where smart cars and automated systems in transportation are expected to launch in the market soon, this automated system will surely influence the public perception of AI.

On the other hand, when Global Positioning System (GPS) is introduced as in-car navigation device, people use this in their cars for finding a path; this provides people a comfortable driving experience because the driver does not need to bother about the surroundings while driving. Besides, it reduces human efforts to remember the milestones on highways.

Another revolutionary innovation in the field of transportation is a self-driving car. As discussed above, a car with GPS assists the driver to navigate the path; based on the data captured by sensors, the car is directed to move on the way towards the destination smoothly after finding obstacles. The sensors are capable of sensing minor objects. It immediately sends signals to operating devices so that, with the use of algorithms working behind it, appropriate actions can be taken by the system. Such cars have set an example of very potent innovation towards the automation of future lifestyles because self-driving cars will be adopted with predicted speed and exceed human-level performance in driving in the upcoming days. It is also estimated that such cars will drastically eliminate cases of accidental death and injuries. All in all, human consciousness will be ruled by algorithms in the near future.

Apart from these, there are many more functionalities that can help humans in the domain of transportation. One of these functions is the Intelligent Parking Assist System (IPAS). IPAS is developed to find the nearest location or parking slot to park your car. The sensor senses the empty parking slots while driving aside and according to that data, an algorithm that is coded to find the best empty slot nearest to the destination, will provide a suggestion to park the car. Again, the question is—Can't we have a good system which relies on human intelligence rather than algorithms?

It is assumed that such functionalities assist drivers, along with boosting safety and comfort. Besides, there are other functionalities such as Blind Spot Monitoring System (BSMS) and Lane Changing. Another tool called Vision and Radar technology were leveraged to develop a system that can predict collision and let the car automatically hit break when it is detected by the system. Machine Learning and Deep Learning are applied to learn about such phenomena and help in finding obstacles on the basis of sensor's data.

Some ethical questions arise while programming the cars to act in situations in which human injury or death is inevitable, especially when there are split-second choices to be made about whom to put at risk (Stone et al., 2016). This way, the power to make final decision remains in the hands of the machine; it can judge whom to save because the machine is having control on both sides. This may create a huge loss, not only to the other driving vehicles in the surroundings but also the entire traffic system. Such incidents might have long-lasting impacts on the society. Being a human, this could always astonish us; how the control has been transferred from one end to another, i.e. man driven vehicles to programme controlled vehicles? But it is believed that people would certainly like to programme their vehicles in future according to their wishes because programming is a dynamic process which can easily be changed. Hence, more sophisticated vehicles may be developed to make human handicap.

Public Safety

Deployment of AI technology for public safety and security in big cities such as cameras for surveillance systems to detect violation of traffic rules and to detect crime has been initiated in the contemporary world. Some metro cities have already started using drones for surveillance purposes; these Machine Learning algorithm-based surveillance systems are useful in predicting as well as finding the nature and place of the crime along with identifying criminals who have committed crime. This algorithms based method is called predictive analysis. Many security agencies are now relying on AI for audio-visual analysis, but one must understand this before justifying anything because one of the biggest problems of this safety process is that it can easily disturb one's personal life. Many places are there in the world where use of drones is prohibited, and surveillance cameras are deployed only after having approval from the authorities. Duality in nature of usage of such devices for privacy is alarming in democratic countries.

Employment and Workplace

Most of the accounting and record keeping assignments are managed by a computerized system in most of the workplaces. One of the prime reasons behind such computerization is speed, accuracy and lesser employee requirements. Many organizations opt for automation of various tasks such as manufacturing, warehouse management, user interaction, transportation, etc. These tasks can be considered fully automated, and thus requires only a supervisory control system. Many other changes in the field of networking, information processing, and searching data have become more intense due to AI. Many services like public relations are also affected by AI; virtual agents are an example of how digital technology has replaced interaction with the people.

AI technology has been proven ideal for mapping all those tasks which are considered as routine activities. Understanding human or natural phenomena under certain conditions has been a major concern for developing a system with AI as it can handle tasks according to the knowledge gathered during the understanding process (training process). This branch is popularly known as Machine Learning (ML). Thus, AI is likely to change the nature of jobs in the near future. It is argued that AI will create new job positions in upcoming years, but it is difficult to imagine in advance what kind of jobs will emerge. It indirectly suggests that existing jobs are at risk; people must find new jobs or develop new skills to survive. This way, AI will directly influence the size and location of the workforce. So, there are chances that it will create new jobs like modern ways to handle the transportation, latest modes of user interactions, novel ways of handling information and creating new markets, etc. Here, the major concern is to develop skill for required tasks. AI has drawn a fine line between low skilled workers and high skilled workers. However, shifting of skills need time to develop; it is not an overnight task.

Entertainment

Growth of Internet technologies is also one of the prime reasons for advancement of AI technologies; a number of people use these technologies in their daily lives. The Internet is enabled to serve a variety of information and entertainment with the use of AI, and most of the time, this information is found viable for the users. Facebook, Instagram, and TikTok are personalized channels of social networking which provide a wide platform for entertainment and interaction. People remain in constant touch with their peers using mobile applications such as WhatsApp and Twitter; such platforms are trusted for audio, video, photos, discussion sharing and browsing blogs. To perform this, the apps are using various forms of Natural Language Processing (NLP), Information Retrieval, Image Processing and Crowd Sourcing which are all based on AI. This way, AI has increasingly enabled entertainment in a personalized and interactive way; people of all the age groups like to work with their fingers on these apps or children are often found happy spending their time with apps.

In fact, there is no harm in encouraging development with a view to make people happy but at the same time it should protect the mental health of the people. Many cases of mental diseases such as depression and other phobias have been detected because of playing mobile games continuously; importance of physical work and physical games is almost lost. Children are disappearing from playgrounds and are mostly found sitting with mobile or other static devices all the time which may gradually ruin youth of the generation.

Education

Education has seen considerable advancements through AI technologies. AI technologies provide face-to-face conversation and learning by developing active agents. Robots and Intelligent Tutoring System (ITS) are also known as expert systems in which online learning is powered by AI. In a true sense, AI has become a helping hand for remote locations where education will not be possible, or instruments are lacking. It is true that learning without a physical teacher may not have good quality, but lacking information and instruments can be satisfied using this technology.

Robots are used to teach some simple and stereotyped functions. Sometimes they are also used to teach basic logic development like in arranging different blocks according to its functions or assembling parts in a game. These robots are powered by AI programmes that work on pre-defined rules.

Intelligent Tutoring System (ITS) is a system that supports human-machine dialogue to solve a problem or to identify a problem. In early days, it was used in a medical diagnosis system also known as an expert system named MYCIN. User is expected to answer the questions given by the system, and on the basis of that answer, the system selects the next question according to knowledge in its database. At the end of the process, it can diagnose the disease, or it may prescribe medicine to cure the disease on the basis of symptoms that were given as input by the user. Currently, ITS is used by many organizations for a range of purposes—for promotion of products, for searching compounds of chemistry, as a guiding agent in museums or as a learning agent for the students.

Additionally, ITS is also used for diagnosing problems in aircraft systems, planning and scheduling, along with financial decision-making, process monitoring and control and many more. Automatic speech recognition agents with NLP techniques are used to find language errors. This way, it helps users to learn a language. Computer vision, a newly introduced branch is useful to understand the image and to identify objects with the use of Machine Learning techniques. A manufacturing unit can also use this visionary system to control quality and manage manpower on the shop. Such systems are deployed in robots or satellite systems.

Online learning system is getting overwhelming responses all over the globe. Recently, Massive Open Online Course (MOOC) is a new model to learn new things using the Internet. Advantage of the MOOC is that any user who is willing to learn can join a course online. Many popular MOOC platforms are from well-known universities of the world like—Coursera by Stanford University, edX by Harvard and MIT, Future Learn by group of universities from United Kingdom and many more. In India, the Ministry of Human Resource and Development has also provided SWAYAM, SWAYAM PRABHA and NPTEL platforms for MOOC-based study. Other online learning tools like Wikipedia, Khan Academy and others are sophisticated learning agents based on AI technologies. Such tools also use NLPandMachineLearningtechniquestounderstand descriptive answers. This way, AI technologies with audio and video content help users to learn and upgrade their knowledge.

Another advantage of AI includes the following: it makes the classroom size larger by multiple users. Users can get guidance from the world's topmost institutes; it is an advantage for users who do not belong to those institutes. Using MOOC, a large number of users get benefitted by learning their special skill-based courses as per their own wishes. This platform using Deep Learning, NLP and Machine Learning techniques to find out users' interests. These techniques are used to learn about user's behaviour, engagements and abilities.

AI researchers have also incorporated a learning system using Virtual Reality (VR). Subjects that required huge infrastructure and real time knowledge like biology, archaeology, marine science, astronomy and many more use this technology for interactive classrooms through Virtual Reality. VR with the help of NLP enables machine translation for converting the digitized documents into different languages, and make users learn the thing in their local language. Hence, these are the benefits for education using AI.

Above discussed are most influenced areas of AI; we will further discuss all with more details and related problems in the next chapter. Here is presented just an introduction of various areas and its context with the AI.

AI and National Security

This section discusses AI and its usage in the military system. In other words, it is about the usage of AI for military advancements across the globe which includes AI-based robotics, Unmanned Aerial Vehicle (UAV), Unmanned Ground Vehicle (UGV) or other such weapons used in cyberspace for defense purposes. AI-controlled machines/robots are powered to fight in physical, informational and cognitive fields.

Military AI and robots are made with many algorithms using various dimensional data. So that, it resembles many characteristics of nature. With the use of Machine Learning, specifically by use of Artificial Neural Networks (ANN), it is possible to mimic a human brain up to a certain extent. Such developments can make the military devices autonomous and enable them to compute in a cognitive way. Though, it is tough to predict how AI-enabled components impact the military power of a country but one can predict from the information that most leading countries of the world are running research institutes of AI and Robotics through their Ministry of Defense.

These days, many leading countries have executed facial recognition systems on large surveillance systems and installed drones like UAVs to detect and attack the target. Technologies for the physical fields include ballistic missiles that work on the principle of 'fire and forget' and similar battle tanks, secretive aircraft systems, rifles and other weapons come under the category of UGV. Such weapons are used to direct and brute physical attack to destroy armoured vehicles, air-ground missiles, bunkers and hidden camps of the army. Another field is informational—an interface between military appliances and data required for precise decision-making. This field is supposed to provide data harvested from the satellite system to the military appliances where it is used to make decisions with very precise scale, to identify a trajectory of incoming missiles and other objects before they are captured in radar systems. The third field is cognitive which is used for information and political operations for disclosing important data or documents to the public as well as to spread fake news about ongoing conflicts by open-source intelligent output. Here armed forces use cyberspace as a kind of battlefield—to misguide people or to hack important data of attackers (Brundage et al., 2018).

On the other hand, it is also believed that it would really be difficult to handle wars if robots are used by nations as their proactive elements because robots are electro-mechanical devices; anything can happen to their mechanism. For instance, a robot installed with the algorithms can give certain commands after identifying specific signals or mechanical devices installed in them may stop functioning. In other words, it can be said that anything can make the situation unsettled for the fighter robots.

All the above discussed military devices and network systems are expected to come into service in near future or it is already working in many countries. Meanwhile, AI technologies are being experimented to make more precise decisions through advanced algorithms. This will boost the decision support system of autonomous military devices as they will not have to stay in contact with human operators.

AI in Informational Field

Compiling a huge amount of data is not an easy task. Researchers were already working on a large amount of data like weather forecasting, satellite information, and share market data. This data was generated from scientific applications and commercial way. Data is in various formats. Another difference between the previous data management and current data management is that it is now processed using AI technologies, where different probabilistic algorithms are applied to make decisions. Commercial data is also becoming huge due to cheaper rates of computer hardware like storage devices and processing devices. Indeed scientific and commercial applications are generating huge amount of data but storage, retrieval and processing of such data is done in-house. Occupancy of data and control of the data is with the organization itself.

In the last three decades, cumulative computerized data has generated voluminous data and it has become difficult to handle. Those organizations which do not have infrastructure and technologies to manage such voluminous data have now turned towards the Cloud technologies. There are very few technology giants which can provide services on Cloud in the world. Organizations which do not have such infrastructure are taking services from the Cloud service providers. Ultimately, data of small scale and medium scale organizations are stored on the Clouds. This will take the control of data to third party. This centralized commercial data (specifically, organizational private data) is reason of concern for the industries and nation as well.

Chapter 2
State of Problem

In the previous chapter, we discussed the evolution of technology along with the current scenario at global level. In this chapter, we will discuss various uses of AI and other related technologies which are very commonly used for speculation among the people to sustain in this era of competition. Just as every coin has two sides, these technologies are both useful and hazardous. Looking beyond AI and such technologies will help us strengthen the core human values. Liberty, equality, and fraternity—the three pillars of a well-functioning society—are weakened by AI. This chapter discusses various drawbacks of using ICT in different domains. Not only joblessness but other impacts are also capable of making persistent changes to the society, human beings and the nature.

In this chapter, we will discuss about usage of various applications that collect data in a hidden way. Many applications collect user's personal data from the Internet platform are belong to social media applications, binge-watching applications cloud-based applications, etc. While browsing the Internet, we find many applications freely available to the users, and the users ignorant about the potential hazards, users happily access such applications as well. Every time, wherever or whenever you click on the content, it triggers the AI algorithms which is running behind these applications. It collects data about your selections. After collecting such data as per one of the parameters of complex algorithms, it is used to predict behaviour of users. The users are considered as products of that supposedly free application.

Many research institutes and academic organizations produce data for the study purpose and make them available within certain domains. Access of such data is a complex process because there is a value of this data, whereas data collected from the above-discussed platforms can privately be used for improvement of various products and services. Organizations may also use them in decision-making process. Sometimes such data is sold for other purposes too. We must try to understand importance of data and its usage behind the screen.

Further sections are about various technology of the current era and its impacts with its typical characteristics. We will discuss the importance with technological

N. Shah, *Artificial Intelligence and Social Ethics*,
https://doi.org/10.1007/978-981-96-8818-0_2

upliftment and society. Further we will discuss its problems in different domains and we will find out crisis of the technology. At last we will discuss about the impact of AI on GDP and ethical use of the technology.

Technological Impacts

In the field of digital automation, the use of ICT is increasing manifold. Let us discuss the leading role of all such technologies, their impacts and characteristics. These technologies are Big Data and Data Analytics, Internet of Things, Cloud Computing, Block Chain and Quantum Computing. Table 2.1 shows the technologies with its elements, impacts and characteristics.

The above discussed technology can be merged with many other technologies of different fields like commercial, mechanical, medical, finance, energy, pharmaceutical, space, etc. Only Quantum Computing is not yet imagined but rest are combined with AI. Implicitly these all are powered by AI algorithms.

To better understand AI technology, it is essential to think about various impacts of its characteristics so that we could come to know about the actual situation of its usage in society. People are rigorously using information technologies in day-to-day life. In other words, they are dependent on them for every step. Developed countries have easy and fast access to the Internet. Therefore, the citizens use such applications for various purposes such as finding locations, purchasing goods, paying bills, reviews, decision-making and much more. It can be said that they are powered by technological force. However, developing countries are not having much dependencies on information technologies yet. But such nations definitely attempt to adopt them for betterment and comfort of their citizens, which is an indirect indication that humans are making their way using this technology. If this trend continues for a longer time, digital democracy would rule the world. Conclusively, it can be predicted where we would reach at the end; all will be far away from the liberal democracy.

Table 2.1 of current technologies with their impacts and characteristics analyse the information to understand the worldview for the near future. In today's time, ICT is in top gear and therefore, many research projects associated with AI and related technologies are going on; many technocrats have predicted future changes by using this technology. The graph presented in Fig. 1.2 indicates upward trend and within a few years it will definitely reach its peak value. However, the only problem pertaining to this is lack of awareness about negative effects among people. In other words, the problems of using AI technology are not yet disclosed. The society is still using it as technological upliftment but implicit behaviour and its impacts are not recognized. To recognize its ill impacts and put it in front of the society will still need some time. In the future, such problems may come to the surface, and ordinary people will realize the issues. Therefore, that will be an enlightenment period for the society. As a result, people will surely change their views about the usage of the technology which may lead towards the downfall.

Table 2.1 Current technology and its impact on the society

Technology	Elements	Impact	Characteristics
AI including ML and DL	Training algorithms, data processing	• Self-driving car • Digital assistance (Alexa/Siri) • Digital face recognition • Human genome project • Handwriting recognition • E-mail marketing • Smart homes • AI-based composer/ artist	• Developing tools using science and engineering for making intelligent machines that can think and learn like humans • ML is a function that can be learned through observation and self-training • DL is a function that can learn from unsupervised data format
Blockchain	Information within block and chain of blocks on the Internet	• This technology is in its nascent stage so nobody knows a stable solution, but it promises transparency, decentralization and immutability • It will provide privacy and security over the digital world	• Blockchain requires implementation of security with a lot of computation power, so it is difficult to implement on a computer network • Public blockchains are difficult to implement because of large data and transparency • For new start-ups, it is an emerging technology because they will not have existing methods and loads but private companies may take a few years to shift to the blockchain

(continued)

Table 2.1 (continued)

Technology	Elements	Impact	Characteristics
Cognitive Cloud Computing	Internet working, storage and services with various platform	• Freedom to use services as per requirement • Pay only for what you use • Lower infrastructure for requirements and cost effective solution • Maintenance is reduced/no maintenance	• SaaS means Software as a Service, a software distribution model in which applications are hosted and made available to customers through the Internet. Examples: accounting, purchase, sales, etc • PaaS means Platform as a Service, provides an environment to allow developers to build applications/services. Examples: storage, networking, deploying, testing, hosting applications, etc • IaaS means Infrastructure as a Service, it provides access to computing resources like virtual server space, network connection, bandwidth, load balancer, etc
Internet of Things (IoT)	Sensors, computer hardware, Internetworking of hardware, processing algorithms	• Smart office and home for energy saving and better security by providing constant surveillance • Better health care through remote monitoring patients • Smart lighting of streets and sensing of traffic control signals	• With the use of ICT anything can be interconnected • Privacy protection and semantic consistency between physical things and their associated virtual things • Heterogeneous devices can work with various platforms and networks

(continued)

Table 2.1 (continued)

Technology	Elements	Impact	Characteristics
Big data and data science	Voluminous data, statistical algorithms and AI algorithms	• Use to derive complex patterns • Use in social media, medical science, engineering, defence, economics, etc • Image and speech recognition	• Applies scientific methods/ algorithms to extract knowledge from big data • It also uses advanced Machine Learning algorithms to predict events related to social, economic and political context
Quantum computing	Different kind of processor that works with light packets	• True impact of quantum computing is not yet imagined but researchers are working on new quantum algorithms and applications • It can be used for factoring very large numbers so it will work for our present cryptography • It may help us to design new drugs, new materials and many new things which are beyond imagination today	• It can also work with SQL and NoSQL (Not Only SQL) databases for large databases • Quantum bit has more capacity than our classical bit that is zero and one • Photons have a unique property called polarization which will be used as an advantage in computing

The revolution of the information technologies will control the world in coming days, and as said earlier, data will be the power. It is important to learn how this power of data has been created, who is responsible for it and who has gathered the data from where? To better understand the future pros and cons of this technology, gradually we will understand through discussion about how all these are important questions. While discussing technology, it is more important to think from the viewpoint of its usages for humankind in general. Most of the time, this perspective of the technology is ignored while doing research in laboratories. It is said that technology is not value bias but usage of the technology is value bias. Is there any way to predict the usage of the technology or can anyone restrict the usage of technology in a certain manner? In today's scenario, it is difficult to control the usage of the technology because everyone wants to use the latest technology in the competitive world and wish to reach at the top. As a result, many people have developed typical mindset that is always engaged in competition, and constantly competing with each other may upset the mental system, leading to breakdown.

Problems in Different Domains

Problem of AI and related technologies should not be determined on a short-term basis because they may provide users ease in immediate mode while using but it can create havoc for humankind if it persists for longer time. I do not consider that it is impossible to understand the future technological challenges. At least for an ICT professional, it is presumable to understand the surroundings and changes that are going to happen due to technology. If we think about AI, Big Data, Cloud Computing and Quantum Computing (if it will be adopted successfully), it is really easy to see the future; technology itself will provide output in terms of future era. So let us think from the perspective of humanism.

Technological advancements are mostly utilized for bodily comfort during leisure time or as a part of recreational activities; very few examples of technological upliftment are made for the betterment of morality of humankind. We can rarely find the use of technology for reducing level of competition among the people, or we scarcely find them useful for solving global problems like pollution, saving water, unemployment, global warming, etc. Rather, it is observed that technology has been contributing to all such global issues. Thus, we must confess that these problems are afflicted by technology.

Yuval Noah Harari rightly said that at some places people are dimly aware of its problems (Harari, 2018). For instance, we are using mobile phones even though we are aware that mobile phones are working on electromagnetic radiations which are harmful. According to World Health Organization (WHO), these electromagnetic waves which damage brain cells can be classified into the category of 'possible human carcinogen'. But people are still using mobile phones very frequently because severity of this device is considered negligible while comparing with its positive aspects such as mobility. Similarly, people are not ready to abandon other such technologies even after learning about pros and cons. It is hard to accept the fact until the masses are not equally affected, such as during the COVID-19 pandemic. People those who are working closely with technology may realize the effects and also understand that the technology which appears as a solution will harm the society in the long run.

It might be true that people working with ICT do not think much about social, political and economic effects of technology. In most cases, 'task is given and task is completed', nobody bothers about the rest. Perhaps it is not important at their level to consider its effects but whoever is responsible must take actions for damaging effects. This is the reason why it seems essential to study the usages of technology in detail in its infancy. It is desirable for each technology to have at least one scientific study with the help of social science and pure science, and to present a visionary output report about the usages and its effects.

Here, we are going to discuss problems of the latest technology in different domains. Some of these are popularly known as a solution but the problems beneath it have not been recognized. Some are indeed evolved as a solution of critical problem but later converted as a leisure for humankind. Let us look at these problems in details.

Problems in Transport

A number of innovations are being done in the field of transportation such as a car without driver, GPS-based navigation, intelligent parking assistance and blind spot detection. Many experiments are made on the highways by companies with a view to provide such facilities to ordinary people as early as possible. Many developed countries are planning to complete the legal formalities for the use of ICT-based devices in real applications as well. Hence, these are going to be part of our lives in near future. In fact, some are already implemented successfully in the society.

Invention of a car without human intervention will be driven with the help of sensors and programmes; actions will be taken on the basis of input given to the machine. Motive of such a car is to provide rest while driving into the heavy traffic of metrocities; it is believed that it will reduce the stress of driving in heavy traffic or it would provide more comfortable rides to the passengers. On the other side, technocrats must think about the control of such cars while launching them on road, and not only about the ease and comfort it provides to the passengers.

Let us think rationally. Do we really think that people in the world suffer from stress while driving car so that autonomous car becomes a solution to help them after knowing its risk factors? Driving a car in a busy traffic may create stress because a driver has to look in front of his vehicle and has to check at least three to five mirrors which show surrounding movements. Apart from that, there are also traffic signals while driving towards the destination on a suitable path. Now, it becomes easier compared to earlier days as autonomous cars can manage all these things using sensors and GPS. However, if we think a little more; when your car control has been transferred to AI-based software, it handles only the sensor's inputs to take actions. Such AI-based software control can be hacked by anyone, or one can take control of accelerator, steering, indicators and all; the hackers who can figure out to manipulate inputs of sensors can manage all functions. Many ICT experts have mentioned about such threats because such hazardous condition could be more dangerous than having stress in a traffic jam.

Moreover, ICT has a bigger role to play; it is also working on a device that can sense signals generated inside your own mind. Is this what a human really wants? If things are going for the sake of medicinal, there are ample examples where technology is used on medicinal ground. Applications like Telemedicine had been developed for medicinal cause in remote areas of poor countries but later on casted for leisure use of material things or bodily comfort.

While working with the GPS, sometimes it may give coordinates that lead to a dead-end. Most of the time GPS tracks you to the fastest way to your destination. Recently, we were passing by a village near the international border of India in search of a temple. With a view to go the quickest way, we punched the destination in GPS because it is programmed very intelligently. Within a few minutes, we started travelling to remote villages of the countryside. The road was not paved, and a little rocky. People from villages were also looking at us very strangely. As soon as we realized our mistake, we first tried to reach the nearest highway, and then with the guidance from the villagers, we could reach a town near our destination. Definitely GPS can find the most suitable path for your destination but sometime you may have such an experience. There are two things to learn, one GPS may provide unusual path and second you are traceable in a very remote area too.

Autonomous vehicles have advanced software that enables them to learn from experiences and update the database while learning from the weather condition, road condition and sensor's input. This way, vehicles are working based on the software made by humans. Therefore, such software containing a bug may result into an accident. Many taxi service companies in the USA, UK, and China are exploring driverless cars. In 2018, a pedestrian was killed in Arizona, USA by such an autonomous car (Gonzales, 2019). The reason for this accident has not been discovered yet but something had gone wrong. Many globally popular taxi service providers have stopped experimenting such cars and have started working on to find reasons for fatality after this incident.

In general, safety is a key concern for people while driving vehicles, whether it is according to the rules or not. Sometimes the other vehicle on the road may not be following a rule and driving towards you. As the driver, you would not want a collision, and find a safe way out. It is not only because you have been taught so, automatically a nerve system follows the social responsibility to save lives. Can an automated car do the same in a similar situation?

There are lots of conversations about communication breakdown like hand signals and voice signals. Hand signals vary from region to region, if a non-standard hand signal is used by any vehicle and it is not recognized by the autonomous vehicle system, this will create a huge opportunity for error (Saudi, 2018). Hand signal recognition is tough in the monsoon season also; many vehicles get into trouble for recognition of hand signals during rain. Similarly, the sound signal may be misinterpreted during rainy season. It may happen that honk does not work properly or the sound of the honk is changed due to rain or water passing through the sound system, which may send a false signal to the autonomous vehicle system.

When an accident on the highway occurs and the debris is littered, front-facing cameras or sensors are not able to find small glass and metal pieces or anything scattered on the road. This could lead to the vehicle with a flat tyre or may lose control due to spilled oil on pavements. Hence, there is a long way to go for an autonomous vehicle to be used in real time applications. There are at least three measures for such ICT-based solutions to overcome; first, it is important to know how they will interact with each other to improve the safety of all vehicles; second, how it will handle the signals; and third, when in crucial circumstances, two autonomous vehicles are in front of each other, then how both will work to avoid accident.

Problems in Privacy

More than half of the countries in the world are democratic. Such countries believe in liberal democracy or constitutional democracy which limits the power of government through the national constitution, i.e. the rules by law.

People of every democratic country want individual independence; wherever they go, whatever they do, or whoever they meet, etc. should be less of a concern for others and government as well. This is a universal right in democratic countries through the constitution. But surveillance systems are watching and recording data about people. Today we find surveillance cameras everywhere—at banks, shops, shopping malls, public parks, religious places, schools, government offices, airports, railway stations and bus stations. The most profound expansion of surveillance systems is dataveillance. Application of this information technology monitors activities of an individual or a group of people by investigating the data trail they leave through activities. It collects the data from every platform such as social media, travelling history, other visits, online purchases and many more. Not only the state or country, even the private firms also have access to a large amount of information.

The process of collecting data of an individual or a group of people for the sake of security is unhealthy for democratic nations. On the basis of customer activities, E-commerce platforms such as Amazon and more are creating sophisticated profiles of customers with high accuracy in their database. This profile can be used for prediction of consumption preferences. For instance, I inquired on Amazon for the 'French Vanilla' once, but I did not place a purchase requisition for it. On the basis of my inquiry, I kept receiving messages for 'French Vanilla' with a good discount scheme even when everything was closed, including courier services, during the period of lockdown due to COVID-19. Most common concern of the gradual expansion of surveillance and dataveillance is that very few spaces remain for us where no one is marking our movements.

When our personal data as well as minute-to-minute activities are collected by a system, it clearly indicates that our personal life has been surrendered to a system. This system has every detail of our personal life like—whether you drink tea or coffee after an hour, which brand of perfume or soap you prefer, who all are in your immediate friend circle, which place you often visit or places where you like to go and stay, which is your favourite food and what not. If you think a little deeply, it also affects your privacy. Privacy is an essential part of your creativity. Such surveillance systems threaten our individual identity in the context of every aspect.

Use of surveillance system in schools or colleges to monitor classroom activity is an odd example. Why are we using surveillance there? Do we want to check whether teachers are doing their job satisfactorily or not, or are students obeying their commands in the class? Teaching and learning both are acts of individual creativity. Similarly, when a person is working at an office, it is because of individual creativity and that is why the person is there; otherwise, he/she would have been replaced by a machine. Students learn in the classroom by their own will. They look at the things differently and imagine the matter discussed by the teacher; it is the students own efforts to learn about the discussed matter. At the same time, teachers can also observe non-verbal communication of the students. At a certain point, they may realize a need to repeat a few concepts without any intervention from the pupils, and can do so by interpreting students' body language in the classroom. Such decisions are made on the basis of their intuition. Body language conveys a lot. Nobody outside the class can realize the same, not even the surveillance system which monitors the class activities. The surveillance system is there to identify physical activities, not cognitive activities. One more illustration can be added here. I saw some pupils in the examination hall—they were not able to write in the answer sheet when the supervisor stood near them. It is not because they were suspicious, but when they find someone watching them, inevitably their mind bothers to look at the activities on the other side. Surveillance system is doing the same in the classroom, apart from sharing this data with other systems to make a dataveillance system.

Privacy of a person in the ICT age is a big question. Your whereabouts have been noted through your gadgets, and liberty of democracy is eventually violated by such systems. Above all, we should not forget that the surveillance system is connected with satellite cameras. The surveillance system is capturing images 24 × 7 with more than one angle. Scott McNealy, the former CEO of Sun Micro system said, 'Privacy is already dead, and we have no choice but to just "get over it" and accept our newly transparent lives' (Manes, 2000).

Problems in Entertainment Industry

Use of Information Technology in the entertainment world is very common but its side effects cannot be ignored, especially on our children and youth who are spending precious hours engaging themselves with technology. If we learn what this so-called 'entertainment' is, we may understand a real situation—entertainment is to adopt new trends to appear fashionable; the key thing here is the kind of gadget you use or ultimately how much you have paid for it. The more you can pay, the more fashionable you are. Information Technology has changed our conventional modes of entertainment like music, cinema or theatre which were affordable to a few people only, but now with affordable cost, easy access and enjoyable quality, it is available for almost all; today all new movies, music, games and web series are available on your palm. Some of the content is free while others are available with nominal charges, and these charges are payable by making online payment in a few seconds.

I can recall my childhood days, when entertainment meant working in the fields, fetching water from the river from all the way to the home, swimming in the river or playing games on the street. We used to work hard while preparing ground for our games and making instruments/equipment for such games. Our daily routine included cleaning an untidy ground which was also used by elders for their work. We used to make clay toys on the banks of the river. There was a lot of talk among friends, and quarrels too, but at the end of the day, we learnt how to do things with cooperation.

Such activities taught us the importance of physical work and community life. There was a lot of walking, leaping and running around to fulfil various tasks. They were not at all easy, they were full of fun; there was no boredom but endless creativity. Even today this is the true meaning of entertainment for me. Entertainment never depends on material things.

Impacts of AI in Entertainment Industry

AI has completely changed the meaning of entertainment in the current era. Before exploring usage of AI, let us see what we do for entertainment. The first thing is Voice Assistance (VA); people are using 'Alexa', 'Ok Google' or 'Siri' for an effortless entertaining life. Second is the Video on Demand (VoD) platform like Netflix which is accessed by many people at their places. Third thing is a flash disk kind of platform to carry large data easily. Fourth thing is generation next—5G data network which will further enhance the speed, quality and reliability to transfer large data like audio, video and images. It has been said that the 5G network is 100 times faster than the 4G network.

Many devices based on voice operating systems such as 'Alexa' or 'Siri' are used for digital assistance, and normally found in home, office, car or hotel. It has been argued that such devices eliminate the need for personal or face-to-face contact. Someone also commented that these devices lead to a community where people will have more conversations with voice assistance rather than their spouse or their friends. People like to play with such devices and often ask 'Alexa, play X music for me' or 'Siri, find some details about Y'. People even give commands such as 'Whenever I am happy, play certain songs for me'. They have many other applications too; these devices can be attached with smart locks or doorbells with the help of other smart home technology. They are also used to book train or plane tickets or buy groceries. Amazon and others have already started their services with voice assistance. According to a research, many factors are essential for the success of voice assistance in digital marketing such as faster and frictionless speed as it improves the sales. There are already more than 4 billion devices in use and it is expected to double in next five years (Collins, 2016). In real life it may provide ease to the users, but while surfing through the data at the rapid speed, our mind will find it difficult to organize data at such speed. It is also difficult to handle within a memory buffer of a device. So for a person who is working with that data, it will create chaos of data on the device and as a human being one cannot handle large voluminous data to select required things among all information in front of them. To handle such large data and make a decision is not even feasible.

Sometimes people also share their feelings with voice assistance saying 'Today I am feeling very lonely' or 'I am depressed'. Amazon and Apple both are frequently receiving such requests. The authorities of such companies have also stated that they are working for solutions—how to tackle such conversations. No doubt, such conversations are virtual but these are only reliable sources for mastering and speedily executing instructions. Such devices rarely commit mistakes as they work based on data fed to them. Though I am unable to find any problem with such conversation because there is nothing harmful indeed, at the same time this is not natural.

In a jungle, animals live together despite their rivalry with one another. There is also a king who dominates other animals, but never heard that animals left the jungle. Their ecosystem is still integrated within the jungle and this is the environment where all survive. There are rare incidents found when animals walked away, if we look into the matter, we definitely find some natural disasters or expansion of the concrete jungle. Animals never opt an unnatural way to survive, they never break the ecosystem and live with the help of one another. As a human being, many live with the above discussed artificial system with no intelligence because a device is never ever able to understand about the psychological waves occurring in its master's mind. A person who is always accompanied by a voice-operated device may have the feeling that she has someone to talk to which seems to be a dreadful condition for society.

Netflix and other VoD platforms have come up with many features. One of the features of Netflix is binge watching where consumers can watch continuous episodes of a series in a short period rather than watching an episode once in a week with advertisements. Researchers said that binge behaviour is an addiction and it also results in deprivation of sleep, lethargic approach, loneliness that gradually takes a person towards depression and obesity (Wheeler, 2015).

Over-the-Top (OTT) platform is gaining popularity in the world of entertainment. OTT means a streaming media service that directly reaches viewers through the Internet. This means that the content of television and film is available to us directly through the Internet on our mobile, computer or TV. Popular OTT platforms are Netflix, Prime Video, HBO, Sony Live, etc. They use Machine Learning algorithms for recommending anything to the user. The algorithm collects data of the people who watch every minute of the show and tag it. Those tags are very wide in range. They also predict on the basis of what the consumer has watched yesterday and how it matters today. Similarly, they also consider the data from a month ago or a year ago to predict how it affects the user's today's choice of a movie. They also compare the data with other communities with similar likes, and the algorithm predicts likes and dislikes of a consumer on the basis of these data. Apart from all these, it stores every platform activity of a consumer like when she pauses, when she rewinds or fast forwards, which day she prefers to watch a movie, what is the location of the watching movie, which device she has used, etc. (Schwartz, 2018). Besides, they also collect the number of clicks on the thumbnails by consumers and rank them for personalized recommendations. Tremendous data has been gathered about a consumer to make a decision for the best recommendation. To continue with the current trends, OTT services will come with new ideas and more complex algorithms. The complexity of the algorithm uses more data about consumers with AI, Data Science and Machine Learning for personalization of movie recommendations.

As we have seen that 5G is much faster than 4G, it will be a breakthrough for Cloud-based gaming where players will not be dependent on the device they have purchased; developers will deliver the content from the centralized servers. Video game developers will have a good market through Cloud, and again, there would be a centralized data monopoly of single owner where there are many video game devices and developers are available at present. Unlike Cloud-gaming, there will be OTT TV in the entertainment sector. There will be only a few number of television distributors that would dominate the market and viewers have to select their favourite show from that. OTT TV with 5G will ease the seamless transmission of data on wireless connection. Apart from that, fields like virtual reality and augmented reality are also powered by 5G. They have offered infinite streamline data to many media companies to plan their next strategies in the competitive market.

There are two issues with 5G; the first is the radiations generated through the electromagnetic field and the other is the centralized power of data and services. Radiation leads towards the health problem of every mammal on the Earth 'as frequency goes up, the depth of penetration into biological tissues goes down, so eyes and skin are main concerns for health', said Dr Andrew Wood of Australian Centre for Electromagnetic Bio-Effects Research (ACEBR) (*Nature Research*, 2019). The second issue is centralization of data that creates a monopoly of a single entity in the market.

Social Media

Many apps are popular among the people around the world to keep in touch via text messages, audio and video. For various social purposes, people are sharing various kinds of data to their friends by using these apps. While sharing data, they become too conscious about others' status and their own as well. A new way has been popular by having followers around the globe; even political leaders are also a part of this. Use of these social media apps for simple data sharing is not dangerous at all, except the scandals like Cambridge Analytica. This company has illegally accessed millions of Facebook profiles and altered their personal political views for the US Presidential Election of 2016. AI algorithms were the backbone in this deception. Commenting about the functions of the algorithms, Halpern (2018) says, 'Psychographic methods bypass "individuals" cognitive defences by appealing directly to their emotions, using increasingly segmented and sub-grouped personality type designation and precisely targeted messaging based on those designations'.

There are other issues related to the uses of such apps; sometimes you may come across an unauthorized or a dummy page to log into your account that generally people do not realize at first look. This will ask you to log in your social media account. Once you log in, it will hack your password details, and then anything can happen; your account and your profile can be misused by some mischievous groups. Another issue is the use of emotional intelligence; though many people are saying that it is for the betterment, it can divide people into sub-groups according to their abilities, skills, locations, etc. On the other hand, emotional intelligence is also applied to target personal likes and dislikes. It means it lodges in your memory and feeds into your decision-making. Marketing and advertising industries as well as entertainment industries are using algorithms to collect the content on the basis of emotional reactions of the users (Hamet and Tremblay, 2017; Forbus and Laird, 2002).

Problems in Education Environment

There are a number of positive and negative opinions about the usage of AI and other analytical or virtual tools in education. If positive points are analysed, there is no need to manage exam-sheets, presence-sheets, mark-sheets and assignment sheets as it simplifies administrative tasks; everything is done by one software, and that is made possible with the use of computerization of the system. Many systems have been deployed to reduce the administration and other paperwork.

Moreover, smart content is another positive note for education. A lot of content is being developed with the use of animation, video and different sound effects which makes content very effective for the learners. It would be, indeed, fruitful for the younger generation around the globe who wish to learn with ease. However, unlike community learning, it cannot be as effective as personal learning. Learning in a community makes teaching process smoother because learners are benefitted by others' ideas and thoughts and can convey their own beliefs to others. For example, one can have all the visuals and smart content of static friction, sliding friction and rolling friction to learn about friction. This content makes them aware about the existence of friction but personal learning with the classmates and teacher is obviously more effective. The reason for effectiveness is not only about experiencing the same by on-hand experiments but also learning various mechanisms used by different students encourage them to learn more perspectives. Suppose, a student conducts an experiment of friction and gets X output while her other class fellow does it in another way and that also produces the same output. Such cases develop their reasoning skills and other perspectives about friction. Hence, community learning is more sensible than smart content-based learning.

Personalized learning is always better to concentrate on the learner's weaker areas of understanding; it will help to identify those areas where learners find difficulties. If we consider personalized learning as an individual growth, it is indeed helpful but this is a very narrow vision education is the motive. It is hardly reachable to the world's view about the topic, and learners might not be enriched by all the views and literature available for the given topic due to time constraint and other limitations of the techniques used for personalized learning. Although the learners can develop their ability in later stages, unlike personalized learning, global learning is really a positive note for education. In the era of the Internet, everything is available to everyone. One can take advantage of expertise through global learning.

Technology Crisis

Throughout the history of mankind, whether the industrial revolution of Europe or renaissance of religious beliefs in Egypt, we have always thought to move forward. If we stuck with one situation or if we lived within our comfort zones, then progress won't be possible. Therefore, moving forward in the field of technology should be considered as a progress; there is nothing constant, except change.

Whenever disastrous incidents took place in society due to applications of technology, people have resisted accepting those technologies. Now, the question is—who can decide which applications of technology create havoc in the society? Let us take an incident of the Arizona car accident once again which we discussed earlier in this chapter, where a cyclist was hit by a driverless car and she died spontaneously. When the case was filed in that judiciary, there were three different entities involved in the accident; first was the car manufacturer who has also developed a software to guide the car on the road. Second was the traffic system, and third was the lady herself. Now, the law is perplexed among these three—whether traffic system regulators or software developers are responsible for such a tragedy. Both are accused of the incident but still it is not clear who is ultimately responsible. This is a good example to understand the risk factors of adopting a technology blindly. If we blame technology, we must learn how things become awkward. This example reflects not only about the technology being used to destroy something but to understand how surroundings are being changed. In other words, people do not have control of the machines which they made to solve the problems of society. In the current century, most of the machines, modified by information technology, have changed the applications and controlling phenomenon. This phenomenon must be visualized by their creators; it must be realized by its investors; and it must be understood by its users. When a creator fails to visualize, realization of an investor is failed along with a user, to resist the use of a so-called advanced machine. How only technology is responsible for such incidents?

The law of co-operation and survival of all living beings is important. Primary education of our society must incorporate such issues, albeit many things are already defined and equality of living beings is known. Unfortunately, we do not know the difference between breeding and nurturing of living beings. In fact, mother nature, the provider of all requirements, is badly ignored by the people. Hence, it is not about technology but it is all about humanity.

People who can afford expensive machines or devices are right now busy adopting new technology for the sake of anything. People who bought it for themselves never ever thought about those who do not have primitive things to survive. If we take the issues of humanity and just not think about the race of advanced technological devices, then we can see that all developed devices are not a necessity for day-to-day life. Human life can exist without such advanced devices. The researchers of such devices have also, perhaps, not thought about its applications in a broader way and that is why after launching a new device, carrying the latest technology, creates uncertainties of its usage in the society.

Ever since people have adopted the revolution of Information Technology, importance of physical work has been reduced. Everybody is running behind the intellectual things. The reason is very simple—intellectual work is more effective than physical. At the same time, a thought without an action has no value. The revolution of Information Technology also brought a warning about other independent associations and enforcement in the society. Mike Ryan, digital futurist and the founder of an ethical

AI company, commented on regulations (interview, 2 April 2018): 'If you look at the history of professions—architects, accountants, lawyers, etc. they study ethics and have accountable independent associations that enforce and ensure ethical conduct. The software industry has no such established models as the industry is too new to have this kind of historic checks and balances'. Well, it is time to form such an association, and many professionals have started looking to the future as well as the way technology affects the society and people. Many such associations are developing codes for specific tasks and distributing them among all without any cost. Such software or open-sources are adopted by people across the world. Many solutions of the problems like hacking data, misused or unauthorized use of data, e-mail phishing, etc. are given by these communities and freely distributed among the users. This initiative is really adorable of developers, but time still demands a controlling body to stop development of such software so a balanced solution can lead the path towards a better society.

As Mike Ryan said, the industry is too new. Many IT professionals might agree with the statement, but the way it gallops is blowing a whistle to everyone in the society. In short, the Arizona car accident should be considered as a line of caution.

Impacts of AI on GDP

Many economic studies have been carried out to study the impact of AI. Majority of studies emphasize that AI will have a significant economic impact. According to the estimates we can say that AI could double the annual global economic growth rates. According to PwC analysis (Rao and Verweij, 2017), global GDP will be up to 14 per cent higher in 2030 because of AI-based devices accelerating the development. It is said that economic uplift is likely to come from productivity improvement due to AI. Many sectors are likely to gain popularity by using AI as its demand is increasing greatly.

The graph (Fig. 2.1) shows the increasing rate of GDP in different countries. China and the US are having more effective GDP increases due to the development of AI technologies. The US is already a developed country and many automations have been done in various sectors. Within the next decade, the growth will increase by 14 per cent, whereas China will record an increase of 26 per cent; China is still a developing nation. So, it is predicted that AI will lift up the country's GDP and will be equivalent to the US after a decade. These two countries will receive more benefits through AI, whereas the countries of developed Asia like Taiwan and Korea and European countries will have moderate growth compared to others through AI. The rest of the countries will record quite less growth because they are still developing AI technology and many applications are in the pipeline, so they have to wait for some more years to see the rise.

According to the study, health care and automobile sectors will have potential AI impact in the consumption around 3.7 per cent, financial services, transportation and logistics and entertainment and communications will have potential AI impact in the

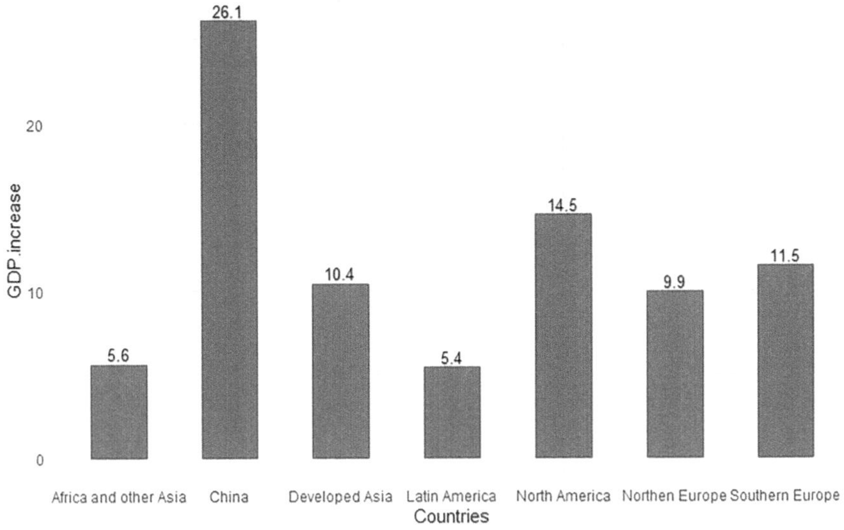

Fig. 2.1 GDP rate increase in different countries (*Source* pwc-ai-analysis-sizing-the-prize-report.pdf)

consumption around 3.2 per cent. While retail, energy and manufacturing sectors have AI impact consumption around 2.2 per cent. Hence, it is predicted that AI has the potential to add 16 per cent by 2030 in the global economy, and as per a report by PwC, AI technologies and applications will increase the global GDP by 14 per cent. Considering everything, AI is poised to deliver good economic opportunities for companies and workers well positioned.

If indeed technologies, such as AI, robotics and automation, are widely deployed across the economy, there will be job creation because there is a demand in sectors that arise or flourish due to new technology deployment. There is also the other side of the picture, the job destruction is also analysed by many studies. This destruction is due to replacement of humans by technology. A 2018 meta-study of results shows (Erin, 2018) the data about job creation and destruction on worldwide basis. Table 2.2 shows data collected from various sources for job creation and destruction.

The effect is likely to be more nuanced, there will be changes in the nature and content of jobs, which would require reskilling. There would be lower-paid jobs that typically require routine manual work which is replaced by machines and jobs related to cognitive skills would be at the highest risk of being replaced by AI and automation. Only skill-based jobs that typically require non-routine cognitive tasks will be in higher demand. Studying the patterns of above given Table 2.2 indicates that job destruction will be at a higher rate than job creation.

The effects of AI may also influence wages, income distribution and economic inequality. There will be a sudden rise in demand for highly skilled workers who are capable of using AI. These people can have gain in their wages, while many others may face a problem of less wage or unemployment.

Table 2.2 A study about job creation and destruction during 2015–2030

When	Where	Jobs Destroyed	Jobs Created	Predictor
2016	worldwide		9,00,000–15,00,000	Metra Martech
2020	worldwide		10,00,000–20,00,000	Metra Martech
2020	worldwide	18,00,000	23,00,000	Gartner
2020	sampling of 15 countries	71,00,000	20,00,000	World Economic Forum (WEF)
2021	worldwide		19,00,000–35,00,000	The International Federation of Robotics
2022	worldwide	10,00,000,000		Thomas Frey
2030	worldwide	2,00,00,00,000		Thomas Frey
2030	worldwide	40,00,00,000–80,00,00,000	55,50,00,000–89,00,00,000	McKinsey

Source https://www.technologyreview.com/2018/01/25/146020/every-study-we-could-find-on-what-automation-will-do-to-jobs-in-one-chart/

Impacts of AI and Ethics

AI algorithms assist to predict about a user's buying habits, favourite restaurants, interest in movies, frequently visiting places, etc. and disclose their private information. This information is used in favour of business by many organizations and raises a question on ethics of the information produced and people's privacy (Sullins, 2021). Similarly, another ethical issue is regarding the truthfulness, accuracy and usefulness of the information appearing from the search engine. While searching on the Internet, different search engines produce different URLs because they are using different algorithms. But implicit standards are not disclosed by such algorithms. Thus, we are unable to know relevant parameters that rank the pages for the result and appear as a result. Machine Learning algorithms are working on reasoning and mathematics; they may sometimes result in mistaken classification because many times learning and predicting algorithm keep secret which makes it so hard to justify the truth of conclusion. Such complexity and hindrances of the algorithm is the resistance in the justification process. Unfortunately, there are no standards about such publications of information but often decisions are made based on it.

There are other examples, such as when you type 'greatest leaders of all time' through any search engine and you will probably see a list of the world's prominent, but most of them male, personalities. Few female names appear. This is an example of gender bias in Artificial Intelligence, originating from stereotyped behaviour of our society. Search-engine technology is not neutral as it processes Big Data and prioritizes results with the most clicks relying both on user preferences and location. Thus, a search engine entrenches these prejudices online.

Any kind of bias should be avoided in the development of algorithms, in the large data sets used for their learning, and in AI use for decision-making (UNESCO, 2021). On the same site we can find another thoughtful example of a painting created by a machine. In 2016, a Rembrandt painting, 'The Next Rembrandt', was designed by a computer and created by a 3D printer, creating a 'Rembrandt' 351 years after his death. Before creating the painting, the programmer had studied almost 346 paintings. Now problem is who can be designated as the author? The company which orchestrated the project, the engineers, the algorithm, or... Rembrandt himself? Many such applications about speech and entity mapping are already in the market. Deep-speaking is a project that convert a voice. Similarly there are other projects which can convert human entity into a video. In fact, this project has been banned by authorities because of ethical issues. AI is also used in judicial systems around the world which raises even more ethical questions. AI could presumably evaluate cases and apply justice in a better, faster, and more efficient way than a judge. Hans Jonas, who has explored implications of science and technology, says 'The fact is that the concept of responsibility nowhere plays a conspicuous role in the moral systems of the past or in the philosophical theories of ethics' (Jonas, 1984). The statement indicates that AI has created more wonders as a supporting technology to pure sciences; when its applications are being developed, computer scientists also carry responsibilities that are self-understood in regards to humanitarian approach. There are many changes coming due to AI and other technology, and some are still in the pipeline; they will change many spheres of humanity. We do not know about its immediate effects as well as long-term effects in the society but it will definitely expand our responsibilities. These responsibilities are for the survival of humankind for the future.

Conclusion

Technology's impacts on the society raises many issues. We have discussed those issues in regards to its domain in the chapter. Incident of Arizona, privacy issues due to surveillance systems, unethical data collections by voice assistance and other devices, psychological issues due to VoD and OTT platforms, scandals like Cambridge Analytica on social media, etc. have had a serious impact on the society and people have suffered badly.

Technological crisis raises issues of laws and its judiciary. Many events took place in the world that need to be restricted but there are loose ends so it is vulnerable for laws and judiciary. The most important matter related to technological advancement is impact on the GDP, we discussed that in AI and its impact on the GDP. In the last chapter we will see how growth is indirectly related to GDP but here we have seen data about different sectors for GDP increase. Hence, it is a major attraction for business.

Last but not the least ethical impacts of AI are discussed that points to the turmoil events. While looking at the state of the problem, we are forced to seek solutions and establish balance among the people. If we look back in history, many leaders had forecast disastrous impacts of technological advancement. They had warned us for various implications and also guided us for what is the best solution. Gandhi was among such leaders. Let us see, what his thoughts about technology and possible solutions are.

Chapter 3
Gandhian Humanism

This chapter will discuss Gandhi's thought on science because science has been inevitably a part of our lives. Importance of science in current era of automation cannot be ignored as it forces us to think about our basic needs which have been changing over the time because of industrialization and introduction of autonomous systems. There are still a few communities living primitively or with the nature, and surviving. It is not that progress in science should not be adopted but maintaining balance in the nature should be our motto. Once again, we need to think of our basic needs and survival of the Earth.

Furthermore, relationship among religion, nature and science has been discussed because many times humanism is considered beneath the religions. In fact, religion was the only motive to live a life in the earlier time. Many religious things are based on our nature. When science was introduced, it was again a search of nature. Science has broken the rules from the nutshell of the earth, people started believing it with its derivable law of the nature. Hence, science and religion both are sustained by the nature. Conclusively, it can be said that religion, science and nature are interrelated, and their importance must be studied to understand humanism.

Gandhi had a vision for industrialization and how manpower gets reduced through it. He tried to explain it by 'non-violence on factory civilization'. Today automation should be considered one step ahead of industrialization as much of the human workforce jobs have been converted into machine-based jobs. Computer Numerical Control (CNC) machine and other latest machines with AI technology like 3D printer remove human supervision because AI made those machines with cognitive task that provides decision support utilities.

At the end of this chapter, there is a discussion about science as 'value neutral' and 'consequence neutral'. We will also discuss phases of consequences of scientific research in the society. These consequences are mainly for two reasons—'manners transformation' and 'matters transformation'.

N. Shah, *Artificial Intelligence and Social Ethics*,
https://doi.org/10.1007/978-981-96-8818-0_3

Gandhian Humanism

Gandhi was not against Science and Technology (S&T) but his vision for S&T for the society was different. Today's machines are products of S&T; various kinds of machines available today to serve the society convert the manual work into mechanical work as mechanical tasks reduce/replace manual work with speed and accuracy. Many tasks are given to the machine for the ease of human lives. While transferring the tasks to the machine and getting the work done is not as simple as it appears before us. It has many adverse consequences for the society, nature and future because ecology system has been violated by machines. Gandhi was worried about the changes that affect the human beings. He had a vision for it and he admired hard work and human energy transformation into constructive work. According to his vision, a judgement on technology cannot be separated from these consequences produced by machinery.

Like a philosophy, science is a process of searching the law of the nature. Scientists like Galileo, Archimedes, Nicolaus Copernicus, Aaryabhatta, etc. tried to learn about the truth of the nature. Initially, it was believed to be a process of learning about our nature and to find its laws for the existence of living and non-living in it. Gradually, these laws had been applied for making new apparatus that work on the Nature's phenomenon. The new apparatus by implementing the scientific rules of the Nature has been a great help in manual tasks and many times these are considered as a solution of complex problems in the society. This way, our science became a generous part of the universe. It has been an instrument to solve the problems of mankind and has raised comfort level in human lives. If this is the truth then where is the problem?

Though today's S&T has become a superpower which can feed the lives and offer them a luxurious living, there are certain issues initiated by it that cannot be ignored. It has hindered human life by simplifying tasks which were believed to be cumbersome earlier. There are certain issues initiated through it. We can divide the problems into two categories: physical and emotional. Though this superpower has played an intense role while making it easy for the physical work, it has also changed a gear of emotions. Let us look how it would affect us as a game-changer in near future.

A voice-based online shopping or Voice Assistance (VA) like Alexa/Siri are the voice assistances that allow ease of communication which have been already smoothened by previous technologies where data input by buyer and receiver process in favour of the details. Voice assistance has reduced the physical work done for input data in the system; now, instead of typing work, buyer speaks on the device and, on the other end, machine also communicates through Chatbot. This is the case of reduction in physical efforts and virtual endeavour for the sophisticated society. Such solutions create distance between humans; the gap of human intervention in the society will be wider and perhaps a threat to the fraternity too.

Solutions given by S&T should not create harmful effects to the fraternity or liberty of an individual as well as the solutions of physical problems should not generate any ill-effects in long run too. The intention is not to criticize or to blame the S&T for many troubles of the world after implementation of technology, but surely to find a middle way for the judicious use of technology. In fact, it is the time when we should use the same scientific methods to analyse world's problems and balance the ratio between human and the Nature. Imbalance in Nature is mainly due to industrialization and after that automation make that process much intense. According to Gandhi, machine should be used to uplift the life on the Earth, he wrote, 'Opposition to mills or machinery is not the point. What suits our country is the point. I am not opposed to the movement of manufacturing machines in the country, nor to improvements in machinery. I am only concerned with what these machines are made for. I may ask, in the words of Ruskin, whether these machines will be such as would blow off a million men in a minute or they will be such as would turn waste lands into arable and fertile lands' (Kulkarni, 2012).

According to Gandhi's vision for humanistic approach towards science, life has propounded a theory that value man-man and man-Nature relationship. Gandhi always prompted the people to cultivate a spirit of inquiry that scientist possess. Gandhi maintained his identity as a humble seeker of truth, but not a scientist (Shantharam, 2016). His approach was to understand science and scientific researches that implicitly shows acceptance of science and raised voice for humanistic approach in usage of it. He was not anti-science. Sambhu Prasad rightly said, 'Based on his critique of modern civilization and the sheer lack of material on his views on science Gandhi has been labelled as anti-science' (Prasad, 2001).

Return to Nature

Science and Technology has not only provided solutions but also gave birth to some serious problems. To resolve such problems, it is required to return back to our origin, i.e. our nature. The simple meaning of 'return to nature' is living with primitives. S&T is the root of modern civilization or industrialization. Latest technologies, ranging from agriculture to medical treatments, are its gift. Its immediate effects can be observed on the lifestyle of human beings which has many barriers. Our lives have been made much easier. However, Nature is being strongly affected by its ill effects because of the way S&T made its path. Global warming, pollution, water crisis, deforestation, etc. have disturbed many natural cycles. Living with primitive things will not harm natural resources, and therefore, it may not break any natural phenomenon. Gandhi and Tolstoy did not profess humanitarian law by advocating S&T, but they taught us to live with the basics and that is why they said that we must return to Nature.

Religion, Nature and Science

Religion is not about faith in God with the help of instruments of specific disciplines. In *Hind Swaraj*, Gandhi has advocated religion not just as a religion but as a religion within religion. There are many similarities among religions and rituals. These rituals are based on science that indicate preservance of nature. All primitive elements belong to Nature and so do the human. Thus, we cannot distinguish religion, Nature and science; in short, they are interlinked.

While urging people to live with primitives, it implicitly indicates equality. Equality in terms of using natural resources is at the top of all. There should not be any special criteria for capitalist, who can only mine (excavation) these resources by paying enough for it; these resources are the legacy of all living beings, not only a small group of people who initially use them for their private adventures and later, to earn money. Starting from digging of rocks to using geographic spectrum for the communications, all come under the natural legacy only. Equality without any bias is necessary. This science for nature has been followed in all the religions. Gandhi had mentioned the same in terms of responsibilities and moral standards. 'According to his moral standards, all men are equal. This is not to be interpreted to mean equality of position and function for all. It only means that, if I hold a high place, I also have the ability to shoulder its duties and responsibilities. I should not therefore lose my head and believe that men with smaller responsibilities are my inferiors. Equality depend on the state of our mind and until our mind reaches that state, we shall remain backward' (Mishra, 2015: 39).

Religion talks about Nature and its value. Many hymns of religious scriptures disclose various facts about the Nature's laws. Some barriers to access these scriptures need to be counted like the language of the scripture is not easy to understand because it is not similar to conventional one. Besides, these scriptures are not easily accessible to everyone, and therefore people find it difficult to understand the hidden logic. As it is not easy to understand by a common man, most of the time interpretation is given by the priests who are believed to be the messengers of the God in the society. Many times people believe the preaching as the ultimate truth without any cross examinations. Hence, this has been a key matter for religion. So, it can be inferred that awareness about Nature is hidden in society. In fact, things have not changed whether it is before Renaissance or after; before Renaissance, whatever was known about the Nature was either through religious scriptures or people-to-people convergence at that time, monopoly of religious priests and their preaching were the final words for the rest. Post Renaissance, laws of Nature invented by people scientifically established a relation between causes and reasons. Moreover, the complex theories and understanding about the scientific law is puzzling for many people. In both the ways, ultimate result is the same. In the game of exploring our Earth and its Nature, everyone should be equal, and just like others, this game should also be bound with the rules.

There are many shades of human behaviour but ultimate nature of human should be a relation between 'me' and 'others'. Simply, what I expect from others, others also expect same from me. According to Kant, man-to-man relationship is the only matter, not God. This gave rise to secular thought where there was a split between religion and facts (reasons). This theme of philosophy indeed made significant shift in society and people were forced to choose a way between religion and reason (science). In fact, this was the time when humans started looking into the reasons for every natural phenomenon. Many rituals are reflection of scientific laws but how many of us are aware of it? In the society, it sometimes seems that practices have been developed to hide the facts; exploitation of people by taking advantage of their lack of knowledge. If everyone equally knows our scriptures and can interpret the meaning or stanzas, it could result in different perspectives but unfortunately, this is not possible for everyone. Gandhi also had professed of the religion humanitarians but he had not advocated slaughter in any way.

There were many forms of superstitious rituals in the society around the world, but enlightenment of philosophy had separated faith from reason. After the Renaissance, people moved towards the S&T where fundamental principles of the Nature was disclosed and a relationship between faith and reason was established. Rituals based on science were surely welcomed by the people and were appreciated when tightly coupled with natural phenomena. In short, such cases strengthen the integrity of science and religion.

Social Changes

As science has started yielding its fruits for the society, people like to find a relation between fact and reason. There is so much appreciation for science by which people have found the law of nature. There are so many techniques invented by scientists which were earlier considered as a miracle. Science has also played an important role to erect natural phenomena of many components on the Earth and within the universe. It is incredible; such as the telescopic invention that helped the man reach to the moon shows the greatness of the science. Hence, it is the root cause for the belief that this is only the future. Many have considered 'science' as solution of every problem on the earth. These consequences are enough to crack myths of religious beliefs with ethics and moral values. It has an impact on economy and politics of the nations. Living standards of humans have become more sophisticated and luxurious, but these impacts are not evenly segregated among the society.

Moral standards differ when power of technology reaches to the people. Apart from money and authoritative power, technology has created a new angle by which world is narrowed down and is controlled from one single point. The problems of manhood with the context of humanism, even in very early stage of industrialization, was uprooted by these power(s). In the beginning of scientific era, scientific research was promoted by special groups in the Western society; people who had contributed to the field of science became a member of such groups in the society, and were also privileged by having the membership of elite club. Science and its applications are mostly developed by these small groups of people. Those who had power were very close to this club and they were used to control its activities.

Advanced technologies like AI and other related technologies lead the moral standards for humanities more towards selfishness and greed because of its control on people's data and people's mindset through it. It is also seen that very few players in the market run the world economy, and revenue is concentrated in the hands of those few people. This could be a major impact for the shift from the religion-based society to science-oriented society.

Countries like India, where religion is a reason for values and ethical humanism is perpetuated with the help of it. Religion enforces feelings of sympathy for every person which is the way to establish equality among people in the society. Gandhi had mentioned this equality and encouraged people to follow religion within religion. Hence, it is desirable that technological power comes with responsibility. If such mindset does not persist in the society, equality will decline and the gap between poor and rich will be wider.

It is also true that complex theory of science and its applications are not understood by every ordinary person, and therefore it should not be the technological monopoly for those who understood and applied it. Today the same pattern as the past is being followed. Priests dominated the society back then and now the difference is that people who had not developed but able to purchase it can have access of the technology. Unfortunately, these are very small groups of people, and this is the reason why the technological power has become centralized and is controlled by such a small group.

Laws of Nature were invented by a small group of people and used as applications in the society. Many times, an ordinary man has neither the privilege to understand nor has any interest (time) to do so. When someone does not know about fundamental principles of science of any application and does not have knowledge about natural phenomena which forms the backbone of that application, they cannot know about valuable resources given by Mother Earth. There are many examples where humans are exploited because of their lack of knowledge. Many times, privileged people have advantage of such a situation and they do not disclose the importance of the resource to their labour or other ordinary people. Many machinery products and raw materials used in various processes are made of primitive elements found on the Earth. Those who know its usability take advantage of others' unawareness.

Gandhi was worried about such an imbalanced society, and this was the reason for his unhappiness and uneasiness regarding industrialization. He was not against science; rather, he was a great scientific researcher for many things. There is an interesting conversation between Gandhi and Rabindranath Thakur on a machine called *charka* (spinning wheel) to spin cotton. Rabindranath Thakur was favouring machines which could increase productivity. When Thakur expressed his misgiving in the year 1925, he complained about people being disturbed in their callings all of which were not without national significance, about the outright condemnation of machines which could increase productivity like in Ireland. Gandhi's answer was '…I wonder after my beloved Sita, the *charka*, and seek to deliver her from the ten-headed monster' (the mechanised cotton textile industry of the west) (Ganguli,

2006: 120). Gandhi wanted *charkha* as a self-sustainable machine that can provide work to people. According to Gandhi's vision, if machine replaces man, poor people will be replaced with machines; as a result of this automation, people who own this machine will become richer which can affect the balance in society. We can see how correct he was at that time. Consequently, social and economic crisis are bound to happen due to centralization of capital.

The usage of the machine has simplified the complex tasks or initiated novel ways for the human lives. Therefore, science has also been delivered for complex procedures in the industries. In the technological era, every discipline is galloping and humans have continuously been replaced for complex, lengthy and risky tasks.

Automation era has two major sides; one, labourers are replaced with machines and the second, skilled people who can work with novel machineries are also short for the factories commissioned with those technologies. Hence, the gap between low skilled and high skilled labourers will widen and many who do not cope with recent technology might become jobless. In the long run, after the automation era, many social and economic problems will erupt from it. I wonder why people at this stage do not realize this. However, a few people could definitely realize the problems of that eruption. Gandhi, Tolstoy and Marx were among them.

Non-Violence

Apart from 'truth', 'non-violence' is another metaphysical foundation of Gandhian thoughts. According to Gandhi's view, *ahimsa* (non-violence) has dragged our conscience and rendered us insensible to a host of other and more insidious forms, *himsa* (violence) such as harsh words, harsh judgements, ill will, anger, spite and lust. All these have made us forget that there is far more *himsa* in slow torture of men and animals by starvation and exploitation because of selfishness, greed and oppression (Ganguli, 2006: 126). Unfortunately, we are not considering such cases as 'violence'.

As tonnes of work get done with the use of machines, cost effectiveness and speed are achieved with accuracy. These three are real concerns for the modern industrialization. In the industries, most of the manufacturing units use machine for production as well as sales, quality control, human resource, etc. These industries are extended by more sophisticated machineries that are run with the help of Information and Communication Technology (ICT) and AI.

Academically, a few disciplines such as automobile, mechanical, plastic and marine came to light when new branches of engineering were introduced due to machines. The impacts of these disciplines have been reflected in the society. These engineering disciplines are focused on learning new technologies of their respective areas, and invent new machines with more sophisticated approach by further modifying with latest research in science. Nowadays, ICT is a supportive technology through which most of the engineering fields take their research to another level. Such research mainly focuses on complete autonomous machines that can work without human intervention. Hence, educational institutes like universities and colleges play an important role in advancement of S&T.

This advancement directly affects the economic and political growth of the nation. International organizations also consider usage of technologies and facilities available in the nation during their surveys to measure the growth of the nation. Though S&T is not a direct parameter of Human Development Index (HDI), it is useful for compiling the information. Use of technology by a particular nation and how many people are literate about the latest technologies is directly proportionate to education. Education is a direct parameter of HDI.

Many such international organizations have been established after growth of science during the industrial era. Trade and market have become global due to ICT development. Eventually, the world started moving towards the material things in the automation era, while missing the values of humanism in most of the index. This was the prediction of Gandhi in the beginning stage of industries and use of machineries. Therefore, he denied the use of machine as it is a replacement of manual work. Today the world runs after technology and its gadgets, whether they are required or not, especially the youth and children are crazy after it. Judicious use of technology is not easy because it has become a key component of entertainment. Consequently, the use of technology will increase and influence both lifestyle and mindset. This trend is further driven by the desire for new and fascinating gadgets.

Gap between poor and rich has always been there if we look back in history. S&T has not made it deeper but I noticed that self-sufficient or self-sustainable nature is developed in human beings with the help of technology that harms the community life. On the other hand, independence with the help of technologies aids people to survive alone, and at the same time, it provides superficiality within a persona; it has less concern with automation era; people who prejudice against others with less technological power as their inferior can generate inequality. Gandhi was against such state of mind.

Another issue is to consider the men in a category of 'resource' instead of a living being; however, S&T has put the men in the category of non-living things. The gap between rich and poor is also responsible for the term 'resource' which serves as a humiliating treatment to the men. People who own a machine, consider labourer as a 'resource' and these 'resources' are available for the machine to work. Hence, it establishes a relation between men to machine instead of man to man. This scenario is completely opposite to what Gandhi expected for the independent country and that is why he was against the use of machine. On one occasion he said, 'You cannot build non-violence on a factory civilization, but you can build it on self-contained villages. The rural economy as I have conceived it, eschew exploitation altogether and exploitation is the essence of violence' (Ganguli, 2006: 128).

Violence on Factory Civilization

The term '*ahimsa*' simply means non-violence; that means avoidance of any form of cruelty with others. Violence on factory civilization is not only due to S&T, there are many other factors that encourage exploitation. When science spreads light in the dark night, it is not *himsa* (violence), when message traverses on the wire, it is not *himsa*, when it is proved our Earth is travelling around the Sun and it is a part of our solar system, many medical issues related to disease resolved by vaccine or medicine, all are not *himsa*. Many hidden truths about the Earth and its phenomenon are disclosed, and all truths of science are not *himsa*. These innovations took a long time, many peoples hard work and sacrifices is involved to bring the law of nature from beneath the Earth. When a law is open for everyone, it is tightly bound with the responsibilities. Science was not the cause for violence, nor it will be; but responsibilities are always there when it breaks the nutshell.

Interestingly, these people work on little clues, like a game of treasure hunt when people are in search of any science law. They start collecting clues while rendering through various places by obeying rules of the game. Similarly, the research should also be bound with rules for the survival of our Nature. Nobody has the right to dig up its resources and disturb the natural cycle. Perhaps this is the missing point in the science era. Humanism also needs to be a rule of this makeover using science rather than just namesake. Renaissance of the West has shown us a path of transatlantic which actually matters for a global humanism, but how to proceed with the scientific era was not reflected then. Gandhi and many other visionaries had tried to emphasize humanism but unfortunately, they were never considered sincerely.

Gandhi was not a conservative or enemy of machines as he clarified his position in the following manner: 'What I object to is the craze for machineries, not machinery as such. The craze is for what they call labour saving machinery. I want to save time and labour not for a fraction of mankind, but for all. I want concentration of wealth not in the hands of a few, but in the hands of all. Today machinery helps to ride on the backs of millions. The impetus behind it is not the philanthropy to save labour, but greed. It is against this constitution of things that I am fighting with all my might' (Ganguli, 2006: 129). If we understand his vision for machines and applications of science, major concern is for labours and their exploitation due to centralization of power owned by few only. Even in the field of ICT, majority are involved in the laborious work, and considered as a 'resource'. This is a new form of factory civilization.

Computation and AI

Invention of calculator had started another branch of engineering that based on computing data. Initially, this branch used to process the data and store them in an organized way with a large scale so that retrieval would become easier. Gradually, these data become enterprise data and started being used for customer relationship management. After 2000, a sudden change was noticed while AI and its applications started deploying new sense of making decision by learning the environment itself.

When AI-enabled machine takes the place of a regular machine, it makes cognitive impacts on the society. Earlier, machines worked on physical task where human labour was replaced now AI-based machines are logically capable of processing data and taking decisions for mechanical tasks. This can eliminate more human involvement which had been an obstacle in the industrial era. Decisions taken by a machine is a matter of great concern. Safety, accuracy and fast processing—the three criteria take AI at a further level of sophistication but 'is it indeed a requirement?'.

Safety of human is an important factor wherever they work, if and only if, use of AI provides sturdy security then it is good; otherwise, replacement of human will turn into hazards.

There are ample examples where AI has reduced risk of human lives. Many complex tasks have been resolved with the use of AI. Hence, two different views of AI are seen for the society: one is philanthropic and other is selfishness. We have discussed both the approaches of AI.

Most of the technological gadgets were invented for the social welfare in the beginning; in fact, they were developed for the noble cause. Lavishness of these gadgets appealed to the commercially inclined world to invest for profit-making purpose. For example, tele-medicine was developed for the people who were remotely located or residing in underdeveloped countries or for those unprivileged people for whom medical help was not possible in person. Later, this product was used for different purpose, it moved towards the commercial path where urban communities use this invention for their pleasure like beauty treatments. Similarly, when a machine powered by AI is augmented to take decisions, with or without human interactions, is good for safety reasons but ultimately, it is paid off by loss of human jobs. Sometimes such new technologies are not affordable but considering it as a symbol of status, they are owned. Such matter violates social stability. Gandhi was aware that social stability does not necessarily guarantee or safeguard humanism independently (Ganguli, 2006: 137).

AI has provided more power to almost all the sectors, thus the control has become centralized and more power has gone in the hands of the owners. According to Marx, 'a form of production where labourer exist for the process of production and not the process of production for the labourer is a pestilential source of corruption and slavery'. Here, the circumstances are one step ahead; the process of production is not for the labourer; machine is everything; and almost nothing is left for human. AI has created a chain of processes that generates fine goods without intervention of men. Moreover, these machines work on fuel, energy, or other natural resources. Capitalists use these resources for their work. Of course, these resources are not infinite, but all living beings have to survive in the world with the finite resources.

All in all, the balance in the Nature is important for the self-life of Mother Earth.

Marx also said, 'Man and nature should be united in the society, so that nature is "humanized" and man is "naturalized"' (Ganguli, 2006: 131). Today's fine products like driverless cars, voice assistant and other similar products do not need human intervention and that is why such AI-enabled products have declined human labour. When AI is incorporated with production units, it makes the production process more intense which is not comparable to human abilities. It is true that many difficult tasks, where human lives are at risk, are done by machine with its cognitive abilities.

However, it is not always possible. We need judicious use of the technologies for the sustainability of human lives.

Value Neutral and Consequence Neutral

Though science is considered as value neutral and consequence neutral, it is true only when it is in its infancy. By the time it starts growing in the laboratory and further reaches the society, both 'value' and 'consequence' are developed together. A matured form of S&T tightly coupled with the 'values' of the society; so, it is important to measure its consequences for the society before it is ready to use. Before reaching the society, S&T must pass through two phases: first, experiments on the novel facts and analysis of the results; and the second, applications development based on the experiments and analysis of the results. Let us look at each phase.

Phase I: Development in the laboratory where experiments to test the facts are on.

Experiments are not only the base for its correctness but also for checking the phenomenal effects in various conditions. This is the preliminary stage when scientist comes across the usability of it for the society. Hence, during this phase scientist can have a vision of its applications. While going through these experiments, social effects of the novel S&T can be measured for the short term and long term. This phase is important to recognize value and hindrance for the social, cultural and economic point of view.

Phase II: Development of various applications using the novel S&T begin in this phase.

This phase is directly connected to the society. After the first phase of the experiments, this phase deals with analysis of its applications and different kinds of use. This process may take longer time. Moreover, the possible consequences related to the novel S&T should be known. This phase also requires involvement of social scientist and economist to analyse its effects.

Manners and Matters

While talking about 'values' and 'consequences' of S&T for the society, manner of the human being also makes a lot of differences. Transformation due to S&T in the society is cultural, social and economic. Capital requirements for the use of such products push forward the economic affects in a more intense way. These effects form the centre of the manner transformation. Revolution of S&T hardly matters in such transformation, but those who own the apparatus, manners have made the difference among others. S&T has created 'power' for them. After perceiving the phenomenon of concentration of 'power', manners are compromised in many cases by capitalistic society.

This so-called 'power' has changed its forms throughout the history and currently, S&T is also changing its form again. Decades ago, precious metals and stones were the form of 'power'. After which land was considered as a 'power' for many years. Industrial era changed that form and established machineries as a new form of 'power'. In current digital era, data is holding the position of the 'power' in the world. Unfortunately, except the capitalist, very few people are able to understand this fact. It is good for them so far; the majority part of their usage is hidden like an iceberg; when something sticks on it, will create huge demolition in the world; manners matter here.

Usage of technology without thinking about its long term effects, may solve the ongoing problems but later on, its evil effects will damage an individual and society both. As Gandhi thought, unless 'manners' fundamentally change and the 'system' is transformed, mere destruction of men, or classes, or institutions will not make any difference; on the contrary, the consequences will be worse as the history of so many revolutions clearly show (Ganguli, 2006: 132).

According to Marx, 'the projection of the social forces of man on to an external power which is an incarnation of arbitrariness and injustice'. Marx has correctly perceived the phenomenon of concentration of external 'power' in capitalistic society. Data in the S&T era has the same status. According to Gandhi, concentration of power as a phenomenon arises irrespective of status, whether it is a capitalist or socialist society, and when it does, humanism is invariably a casualty. If humanism in the sense of human dignity and freedom is violated in the process of eliminating human alienation, the employment of unjust means leads to an unjust end; not the just end of humanism (Ganguli, 2006: 130).

As S&T is growing, matters also change for human accordingly. S&T has played an important role to strengthen independency of an individual. Many tasks, which were barriers for a single person, now can be done without help of anyone. A strength of independence is always there when S&T is used for impersonal work. In fact, this is also true for a small group of people or a single community; further, it strengthens the city, the state and the nation as well. When nations are living with the power of S&T, it affects the international reputation also. On a positive note, nations became more sustainable; there will be a change in mortality index, poverty index, hunger index and many important issues related to nation's growth in context of the world. Nation will improve but certainly there will not be improvement in humanity. These technologies will also be used for defense, making new weapons, increase the crime or change the mode of crime. It will strengthen the espionage system of the nation that will lead to other difficulties.

On the contrary, this will also give birth to invisible competition among the nations to establish their supremacy. The race of 'super power' among the nations matters a lot for the peace of the world. This can be clearly understood by taking a look at the cartoon published in *The New York Times* in October 2014 (Fig. 3.1).

The Cartoon with an Article Titled 'India's Budget Mission to Mars' in The New York Times

Fig. 3.1 The cartoon with an article titled 'India's Budget Mission to Mars' in The New York Times (*Source* https://www.bbc.com/news/world-asia-india-29502062)

Conclusion

Invention of bio-chemical equipments, development of sophisticated detective systems and biological research against the Nature shows the red signal for human lives if the defense power is closely looked at. These are man-made threats, and destruction caused by such inventions can demolish world multiple times. Just want to conclude by Gandhi's sharp line of demarcation between 'living dangerously' and 'living in the face of danger'. According to him, 'there may be sensation in living in face of danger and living dangerously. A man who dares to live alone in a forest infested by wild beasts and wilder men, without a gun and with God as his only help, lives in the face of danger. A man who lives perpetually in mid-air and drives to the Earth below to the administration of a gaping world lives dangerously. One is purposeful and other is purposeless life'. He concluded 'let us live in the face of danger'.

Chapter 4
Automation and Humanism

Automation, the newly introduced branch of technology, is going to revolutionize almost every industry by increasing productivity using AI, ML and DL. Simultaneously, Robotics also play an important role in the growth of manufacturing and health care sectors. The increasing number of adoptions of automation-based technology in various sectors will further lead to economic benefits. While looking at the impact, multiple negative and positive aspects are observed, however, they are not considered in a balanced way. Stephen Hawking, Elon Musk, Bill Gates, and many other techno leaders and scientists in this industry had expressed their concerns about the risks imposed by AI. Many AI researchers also supported them because they, as researchers, indeed had a vision of future role of AI in human lives. At the same time, it is our duty to emphasize on improvement of the negative aspects of the technology with a view to balance its effects. Therefore, it is necessary for many people to contemplate on this issue.

In human–machine relationship, AI and related fields are not only the points of concern; there are many other technologies which have made differences; they may have created indirect impact rather than direct impact on the society. We should also discuss these technologies and their impacts.

Being an optimistic, I can mostly think about positive effects of technologies but all of those might not be true at all. Therefore, it is important to discuss about both the sides. In this chapter, we will discuss automation with humanism because all of us are using AI and other emerging technologies in various ways. We will revisit problems of the Internet, Cloud Computing and IoT along with discussion of the ethical issues. In coming section, we will discuss the real problems. We will also discuss changes in policies with respect to AI. This way one could find the common space to understand the problem and also integrated with different entities of the society.

In the beginning of the chapter, there is a discussion about its myths. Many researchers, philosophers and social workers resist the use of excessive technology in daily life. Despite their warnings, no major changes have been noticed in real

N. Shah, *Artificial Intelligence and Social Ethics*,
https://doi.org/10.1007/978-981-96-8818-0_4

life. Rather, usage has been increasing consistently with the arrival of new trends and technology in the market such as 5G and upcoming 6G network. A particular government or social institutes only are not responsible; every human being is responsible for such changes. Defining policies for the usage of technology in regards to legitimacy and ethically caveats show the future trends and required technology for human welfare.

Many times, we have noticed the myths about the advancing AI and where it will take our future. There are many examples where AI technology has been considered as a disaster; but we will not be able to find its place until we explore the facts. Whatever the myths, one should know them, and society, being a pioneer of livelihood, must present correct scenario by studying pros and cons. AI has been adopted for many reasons and many states have switched over to it for development using this technology. When world is moving towards it and present generation is using most of the gadgets that are powered by AI, one cannot deny its future. Hence, learning this technology is a necessity for everyone, but role of everyone for learning should be well defined.

We also need to consider stakeholder analysis for deploying new technologies and to have a broader view on impacts on the society. In the chapter, we will discuss stakeholder analysis for technology used for automation with the context of society and its role. Our society is based on the Nature of the Earth and we should differentiate it in the four Es of Ethics, Equality, Equalitarianism and Ecology. The ultimate goal of every research is to provide healthy and happy living for all. This is the study about the outcome of technology in context of society and humanistic approach for long period by considering these four 'Es'.

Misconception of AI

There are many sensitive issues related to AI and its applications; some may show its affect in the near future while others may have long term effects which will be on our future generations; there may be very narrow scope to alter them for human welfare. Short-term effects may come on the surface within 2–5 years and long-term effects may be seen after more than 10 years; however, we cannot perfectly predict them immediately but we can gradually determine its effects. Sometimes people do not consider the technical aspects as a whole but develop prejudice on the basis of so-called 'things' uttered by others. Hence, this section is about its myths and why we need to learn this technology. Discussion about myths will clear the air about misconception of AI. It also helps us understand problems which is indeed required to think its indirect effects to the society and its implicit mechanism which is hidden.

While working on AI, many myths related to its routine usage and other unnecessary fears among the people came to light. So let us first identify what are these myths.

Myths

Super intelligence come with AI and it will take over human intelligence. There will be no role of human expertise and intelligence.

AI is both science and engineering; with computer intelligence, it helps to understand pattern recognition, natural language processing, decision-making, and problem-solving and learning from the environment. There is no specific single intelligent agent that can solve all kinds of problems. In fact, researchers are using divide-and-conquer method to separate issues and apply solutions using AI as per different applications. Till now there is no single AI application that can solve each problem in the environment. A few specific AI applications work in given a environment only; hence, AI is the inter-disciplinary area of study with many sub-areas. Figure 4.1 shows the majority areas where AI deals to solve the problems.

Super intelligence is a tricky field; even researchers are not sure about it, and besides, it is not a definite term. One should not be scared because it is ultimately a man-made machine. All the programmes and applications are run by multiple algorithms developed by humans. Human intervention is required since it is not working with the sense and emotions like humans that help to make decisions. AI or any subset of AI like ML or DL cannot replace humans. It helps to make decisions where humans cannot do because of limitations of their abilities. It makes the process fast and accurate, hence, decision-making is effective. Sometimes it makes decision by learning from the environment but learning agents are developed by humans.

Another myth about AI is that Machine Learning and Deep Learning are automatically learning systems without human intervention.

Typically, Machine Learning and Deep Learning are demonstrated as magical methods that automatically learn about environment and take input itself to provide best justifiable outcome. It is true up to some extent if all data is fed in the system, and there is no new knowledge outside the system which is next to impossible

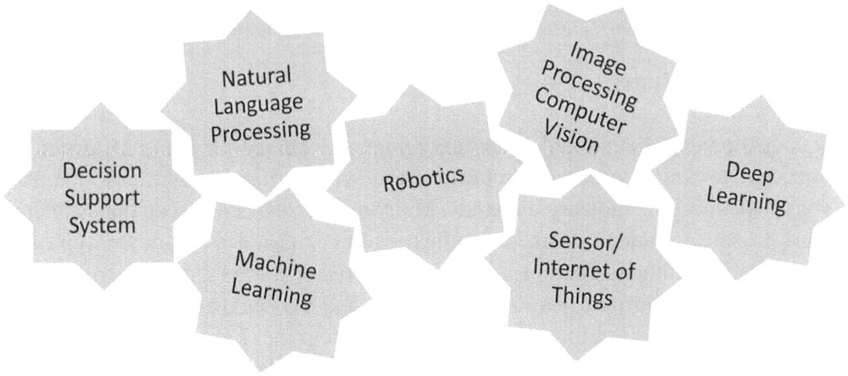

Fig. 4.1 Various areas of the artificial intelligence

because the world is generating new knowledge every day. To impart this knowledge in the system, multiple data sources are needed from the environment and human intervention too.

In fact, Machine Learning and Deep Learning are methods that perform a lot of cleaning and scrubbing activities on voluminous data. Machine Learning trains the system to understand nature of data to take better decision using many statistical methods. Deep Learning usually has multiple layers of neural network; mostly for the audio, video and natural language processing. Here, algorithms depend on human skills for very large data, we require fine tuning of data collection that need to be rightly labelled by humans to train such system.

Role for the Needs

Considering the ICT era so far, many researchers have found that AI will be the future; at this point, I do not deny the prediction, but at the same time, it is advisable to follow the remedial tricks to reduce the severe effects. There are certain roles for everyone in the society so that we can develop a herd solution that is expected to provide relief not to only certain level of people, but to everyone. Individuals, education institutes, businesses and government are main entities to understand its importance. Here we are discussing their roles.

Technocrats

Primarily, it is the responsibility of individuals to keep themselves updated by continuously learning and evolving with the market dynamics to pace with the technology upgrades; individuals should build adaptive capability so that one can learn and relearn new tasks with the changing environment.

Educational Institutes

The educational bodies should not entirely migrate from their traditional curriculum to incorporate coursework, but should work in synchronization with new age technology and emerging industry demands. Many times, it has been seen that academia prefers to select subjects from the industries but it is not a top-down approach; curriculum designing is a bottom-up process which is designed according to students' capacity and their current level of knowledge, and expected to be taught as basic subjects that are required for foundation of any discipline. Later on, advanced technology can easily be learned. Therefore, academic institutes should collaborate with industries so that they can work on reducing the gap; seminars or workshops can be arranged by industries so that students get hands-on industry experience by working on a range of real-life challenges pertaining to current technologies and practices.

Besides, a continuous skill improvement system is also required so that young minds can be taught to adapt themselves from an early stage and learn to transfer their skills according to their job landscapes.

Businesses

With the increasing percolation of AI within organizations and adoption of new technologies, on-the-job training is believed to take a vital role for transition of people into new roles. Organization's human resource department will focus more on improving the employee experience across the workforce. It is possible that man is used as a toggle mode and there is continuous switching among the task, which is indirectly harming the humanitarian approach. Try to avoid such circumstances where employees are very uncomfortable.

Government

AI-driven automation is likely to have a huge adverse impact on low-level and middle-level skilled people employed in an organization. Government is responsible to upskill the population so that difference between job availability and employee readiness can be balanced. Middle-level skilled and low-level skilled people should be provided with a basic training to perform the tasks using computers and AI-driven tools. Apart from that, they must be trained in basics of computers. The government should nurture a culture where academic research and industrial implementation coexists, and benefits each other.

Current scenario is making the role of academia and government more critical even though progress in AI might be aligned with meeting the needs of business and individuals. AI-related courses and trainings should be incorporated with the conventional teaching, however, at the same time, ethical issues related to same should be a part of it.

Government should consider its malicious usage that one cannot stop it; rather, such things will be a major setback for everyone. They must learn about the future technology or about the future changes along with its effects on political, economic and social paradigm shift. Government should also consider the progress of AI-enabled technology seriously for two reasons; first, to cope with the global market trends because synchronization with the development is a necessity for any nation, second, there is a dual use of technologies so awareness about them will guide us in understanding its complexity against malicious usage.

Automation with Humanism

Many organizations are developing application of AI for higher level of automation. Some are indifferent about future or long-term effects of automation. Perhaps their present crisis pushes them towards it. Automation will provide lofty gadgets, and the power of the technology that glorify their present will help them to access all worldly material things. Such approach is alarming for the future. Physical and manual work is almost declined in this technological growth. Man to man communication is also resisted when people use chatbots or VA.

The trend of centralization of data and its processing breaks the decentralized work on which villages have survived. Gandhi feared that if the state was made accountable to the distribution, it would monopolize the means of production, and that would inevitably lead to concentration of wealth as well as power in the state (Mishra, 2014). In short, he was realistic and prepared to accept industrialization with some reservations. He said, 'No one is opposed to modernity but opposition to its misuse of its excessive use' (Kogle and Shreekumar, 2011). This indeed pauses a question of human approach towards their life, their future and the environment. Even after providing solutions of complex problems, it is the root cause of certain issues as we discussed earlier even though finding the evil in usage of technology is based on humanism.

Expressing about the roots of evil, Gandhi said that views of *ahimsa* has dragged our conscience and rendered us insensible to a host of other more insidious forms of *himsa* (Mishra, 2015). Greed is one of those forms. Since people are inevitably crazy after technology, their greed for achieving name and fame by using latest technology become higher and higher. As per Gandhi, the vicious circle of greed, exploitation and violence can only be broken by the practice of ethical principles of non-possession; otherwise, it will invite a bloody and violent revolution (Mishra, 2015).

To avoid violent revolution, we must think about our present and future. The worldly material things for which people are crazy in our present and future is hidden beneath it. To realize our present, we need to pull it out of the darkness of greed, exploitation and violence. When we start working on it, we face lots of conflicts with in the self and outside world. In a reality nobody wants to get into such conflicts. How can have acknowledgment of conflicts without realize it within? To find common grounds of the conflicts, one should understand human–machine relationship. We will discuss about the ratio of human and machine in the automation era in the coming sections that highlights some scenarios where work is ready for labour or labourers are ready for the work.

To bring conflicts on the surface, we must deal with the problems of the society and the living beings. There are many incidents where some problems appear on the surface but are not acknowledged, and slowly disappear without any significant causes. People tend to forget such issues after a few days or there may be some implicit understanding to not pertain the issues more in the public. This kind of diffusion of close working people or society to become a group of similar goals without ethics is a root cause to resist conflicts. This diffusion makes tightly coupled effect where it is difficult to find its loose ends; in other words, the greed of human plays an inevitable role to commission self-centred society. People are exploited by such a small group because they have created a power by mutually understanding with one another within their group. Gandhi had also mentioned such things with respect to countries. He said, 'Industrialization is, I am afraid, going to be a curse for mankind. Exploitation of one nation by another cannot go on for all time. It depends entirely on your capacity to exploit…'. This will take world towards the bloody and violent revolution which is predicted by Gandhi and other philosophers like Marx. Gandhi advocated state ownership, where a large number of people have to work together. According to him, society should be empowered by co-operation where moneyed men should play a leading role on the basis of non-violence. He insisted upon revival of rural industries where raw produced are converted into marketable products. He dreamed about self-contained villages that manufacture useful stuff and make villages self-sustained rather than used as a means of exploitation (Joshi, 2002). According to him, humanism should be developed in the society this way. Gandhi believed in trusteeship; he attempted to establish it as a creative application of the 'science and non-violence' with concern of economic sphere. He was worried about widening the gap between the rich and the poor in India. He bluntly said, 'A non-violent system of government is clearly an impossibility, so long as the wide gulf between the rich and the hungry millions persists. The contrast between the palaces of New Delhi and the miserable hovels of the poor, labouring class nearly cannot last one day in a free India in which the poor will enjoy the same power as the richest in the land…. A violent and bloody revolution is a certainly one day unless there is a voluntary abdication of riches and the power that riches give and sharing them for the common good' (Gandhi, 1945).

Today's society is far advanced than the society at the time of industrialization because people are turning their mechanical works by autonomous machines where less human intervention is needed. We can see that self-centred society never allows the conflicts to be on the surface. Automation certainly affects the people, and several times, incidents come before us such as denying use of the latest equipment. However, it is disapproved by one or another reason, an example is the incident of Arizona car accident. Another example of technical issues where AI algorithms learn and predict about people's personal and confidential details, and fetch data from their social media without their concerns are the best examples. Acknowledgement of such conflicts must be addressed in the society with keen public interest during open public forum. Society needs certain organizations which can set the standards to be followed by industries and developers. Elon Musk, the Founder, CEO, and Chief Engineer at Space X, also advocated for the regulation in AI. He also warned the world by saying 'AI is more dangerous than nukes'. This blank need to be filled as soon as possible as it also looks upon ethical practice of automation, specifically in the field of ICT to identify problems faced by people and its long-term effects. If steps are not taken within the right time span we cannot stop the above said violent and bloody era.

Sharing Space

While working on the issues, we need to find out common grounds among the people who are involved in ICT and related technologies at various stages. At a first glance we can divide them into three categories: first category is of those who are interested in use of a technology as a product; the second category is of people who are working for this technology as a developer; third category is of people who are directly or indirectly affected by the use of this technology and its popularity that can change their surrounding world. Figure 4.2 shows the diagram of their integrity and functions. While looking little deeper, we can find further sub-categories of users by considering their purposes. People who are interested in using the latest technology for the automation might have three purposes; first, they want to enhance their production and revenue in the competitive market; second, people who are using the technology for entertainment; last but very important, those people who use the technology for the research in their fields. For example, ICT is used in medical science, space science, bio-chemistry and other many areas to solve complex problems. By the way, very few people come under the third category; next to them, the second largest community is manufacturer or the people who use this technology for the power. The largest community is the users of ICT to satisfy the purpose of entertainment only.

Developers who are also known as coders, develop programmes and design an interface between any kind of hardware and software. Their work is based on their job that is mainly for their survival. In the era of high competition, their skill must be worth of coping with the latest technology and that is the reason they are learning and dealing with automation technology. These people are very much aware about

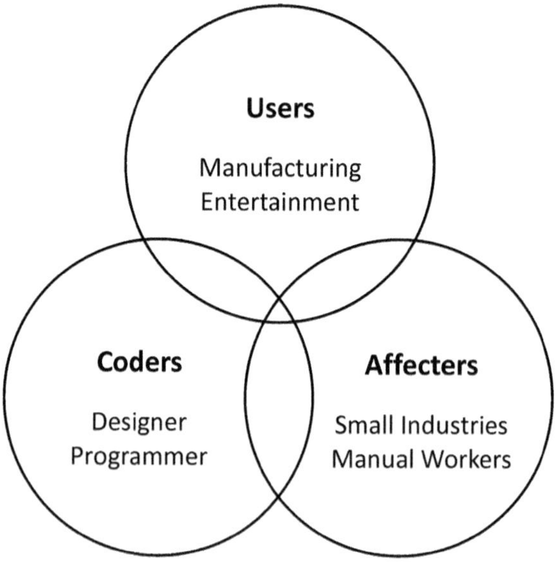

Fig. 4.2 Integration of users, coders and affecters among each other

upgradation in ICT; if they are not, there will be great trouble for them in surviving this domain. There is always a fear of loss of work or downgrade in work profile due to inability to adopt new technology. Hence, they do not have any control on the entire developing chain, if at one stage they find the way is not suitable for society or it will be harmful for future generation, their vision is considered as baseless.

Figure 4.3 is about environment and society for ICT, where four entities are involved in the process of automation—industrial units, research institutes, developers (coders) and users. Relationship among the entities has been shown; where industrial units sell its novel products to the users which are either solutions to earlier incompatibilities or something new has been evolved by researchers. Upon a successful application of their new ideas, it is given to the developers for making new approach by incorporating it into their products. Developers make fine product which is sold by the industrial units in the market and as said their role is a kind of labour. Hence, their vision is not important in entire chain. We can find integration of first two categories of people who are sharing space on technological plane, but affecters are missing. In fact, their issues are not considered seriously, neither society nor government is paying attention to them.

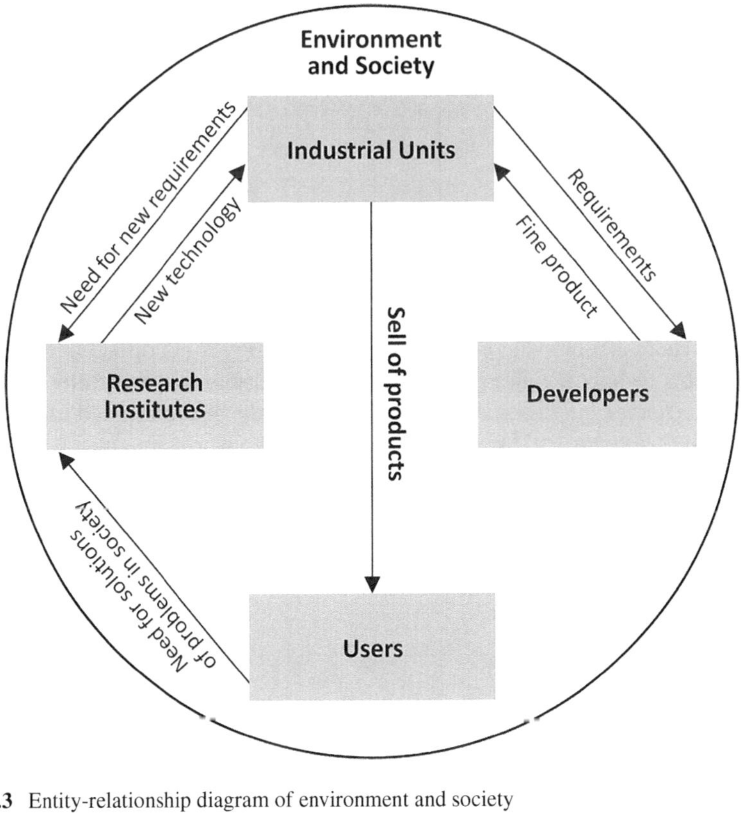

Fig. 4.3 Entity-relationship diagram of environment and society

Affecters are unable to find alternative occupation after automation. Their main occupation is destroyed due to technologies. Gandhi commented about such unemployed or underemployed people of India saying, ‘It is not to find leisure for teeming millions inhabiting our country. The problem is how utilize their idle hours which are equal to the working days of six months in the years. Dead machinery must not be pitted against the millions of living machines represented by the villagers scattered in the seven thousand villages of India’ (*Harijan*, 16 November 1934). His view has relevance in the current time as well. Today not only villagers but urban people are also workless due to automation. Gandhi with Marx and Engels pointed out that it is the system of capitalism at the root through which the machines are begetting the evils.

After looking at sharing space of automation and mapping it with the industrialization, we find that it has no concern with parallel society where affecters are struggling for the survival. This is an important parameter while moving towards changing the system for humanitarian approach. It is indeed difficult to find correlation between automation and its needs for the society. This is more like a walking belt without considering the need or requirement of walk. We find very little integrity with demand and necessity. Each entity is working separately by having its own vision. Weaving a net to get them together requires integrity among all, if one entity is producing some output, it should be an input for another entity. This way, the cycle of the automation needs to be generated like other cycles of our nature.

Issues

It must be admitted that automation does create issues, however, all the issues of society are not created by automation. Indeed, we are trying to address ongoing challenges with the help of technology but act remains fundamentally ethical in character. There is room where AI and other technology is not directly involved but power of this technology along with the responsibility is missing. Rajiv Malhotra, author of *Artificial Intelligence and the Future Power*, also discussed many issues regarding it (Malhotra, 2021). Problems that shake the world are given below:

- Human Security
- Joblessness
- Inequality
- Ecological Changes

Human Security

Social media, or many applications like WhatsApp, TikTok, twitter along with such other online free applications are examples where user’s data have been leaked for other purposes. It has been said that the user itself becomes a product when any product is available on the Internet without any cost. While using such products or working with them, people are unconsciously constantly transferring their private data.

Another major loophole for the human security is CCTV cameras and satellite monitoring system. Albeit, it is not completely on ICT system, but data are captured by systems without knowledge of a person. This kind of data-gathering makes human security and privacy vulnerable.

Sophisticated cyber operations and emerging technologies are used for cyber crime. Many researchers believe that AI is used and will be used for more such cyber attacks, however, no such documented evidence is available yet. Besides, it is also considered that AI and ML together can lead the foundation of cyber-security and strengthen the system but now these systems are performing poor against human security.

Furthermore, physical attacks with the help of weaponized robots like drone have been developed. For example, Iranian military leader Quasem Soleimni was killed in a drone attack in April 2020. The point of concern is that necessary defences for such attacks are capital intensive, and the hardware and software required to conduct the attack are widely distributed.

AI and emerging technologies change the nature of communication in the society. ICT is playing a major role by affecting political, social and economic way because role of social media in elections, protest movements, buying habits of a person, their whereabouts, etc. are influenced by AI. Social media technologies allow agencies to monitor sentiments and attitudes. Research suggests that social media strengthens incumbent authorities' regimes as incumbent governments can handle the information available in public view. Social media 'bots' are also examples to spread political messages and cause difference. Apart from this, automated spear phishing has demonstrated that automatically generated text can be very effective to make people fool and this way shaping a public opinion is successful (Brundage et al., 2018).

Joblessness

It is true that AI, ML and robotics are potential technologies and a key to increase productivity in advanced economics of countries like USA, EU, Japan, and China. On the other side, it could also produce lots of disruption; a study says that nearly 37 per cent of workers were worried for their jobs due to automation (Brown et al., 2018). In short, almost every sector is equipped with the advanced technologies and automation is accepted as world of tomorrow. Consequently, many types of machineries at work and people are being replaced by it. Choice of the machineries has some root causes—precise work, speed of the work and easy management.

There are surveys where participants believe that AI will help humans to solve complex problems as assistance of the AI over the human is preferable. Obviously, such surveys have been conducted on educated people, those who know something about this technology. People those who are layman and not much educated or working on daily wages are not involved. In process of such a survey, everyone from each level of a society must have their voices.

AI is also transforming workplaces; earlier, human resource department was responsible to cast their point for a candidate on the basis of curriculum vitae in the selection process; now, there are AI algorithms to analyse a candidate and generate score. Many companies are working with such algorithmic solutions because they are unbiased systems. Financial services and other related services are also using technology for automated entrance papers or creating PDF invoices into computer systems. This way, the work of entry-level workers as well as clerks is automated by such technology. Similarly, transport services, construction sites, health care sectors, accommodation and food services, manufacturing, etc. are also using AI as a smart and sophisticated service solution. It is now realized that benefits of automation outweigh the labour-cost substitution.

According to a case study in the International Federation of Robotics, it is evident that one more robot is replacing the employment of about 6.2 workers and one more robot per thousand workers can reduce wages by 0.73 per cent. With time, more sophisticated robots are being prepared and more work is being transferred to them. Hence, more reduction in employment and wages cannot be denied.

Inequality Among the People

There are many consequences of automation for the organization on account of work, these include activities performed for a given task, skilled work for the automation and cognitive work due to automation. At low level, with use of robots, most of the stereotyped activities can easily be automated by computerization. So, those works at the ground level or manufacturing tasks usually done by the use of tools or machineries are now replaced by fully automated machineries or semi-automated machineries. When such automation takes place, requirement of skilled workers for the machineries rises and most of the organizations demand for people with knowledge of current working technologies. Thus, demand for skilled workers creates hike in their wages. Third category is for cognitive task: workers who merely execute tasks based on rules but they do cognitive processing of data or information generated from data. These are very high-skilled people with very high wages too. In short, there is a large difference in wages among highly skilled, averagely skilled and unskilled workers.

If we consider the effect of robotics given by International Federation of Robotics (IFR), unskilled workers will have concentrated effects due to this replacing technology as there are also some evidences that affected men take jobs from women in some occupations (Acemoglu and Restrepo, 2017). Averagely skilled people have been in demand due to their knowledge of working with current technology but as soon as industries are upgraded with new technology, present skilled people might get replaced by others or they have to develop their skills for the latest technology.

While considering the high skilled people, there might be very less effects of this automation.

Work for Labour or Labours for Work

In large warehouses, manufacturing shops or shipping yards, the work with high degree of computerization within the organizations is always in the pipeline; the output of one segment is immediately transferred to another segment. Hence, it becomes an input for other segments; we hardly see any human in this chain of work. When humans are part of such automated plant, they are mainly found busy doing stereotyped work; they need to be attentive to the workflow of the chain; even a single skip in the chain will disturb the entire work. Hence, it is a kind of things where labour is ready for the work.

Another scenario, where a potter or weaver or a dyer (who dyes the cloths) is working in batches. Raw material is available and necessary pre-processing is applied to prepare finished products; one can start towards making fine goods by processing on it. Most of the time such work is done by hands and it is done by single person or a group of two to four people (mostly other family members). Here, this is how work is ready for the labour.

In the paper by Acemoglu and Restrepo (2018), they have developed a model of automation, tasks and the demand for labour. They have used their own task-based framework which was published in 2016 where aggregated output is produced by combining the services of a unit measure of tasks x belongs to [N-1, N], according to following Cobb-Douglass aggregator

$$\ln(Y) = \int_{N-1}^{N} \ln y(x)\, dx$$

where ln(Y) is aggregated output and ln y(x) dx is output of task x in a complete process.

If task produced by human labour = l(x) and task produced by machine = m(x); then

$$y(x) = \begin{cases} \gamma_l(x)l(x) + \gamma_m(x)m(x) if\ x \in [0, 1] \\ \gamma_l(x)l(x) if\ x \in [1, \mathrm{N}] \end{cases}$$

where γ_l(x) is the productivity of the labour in task x which is assumed to be increasing. γ_m(x) is the productivity of machine in automated tasks which is static or decreasing.

According to the equation it has been assumed that γ_l(x)/γ_m(x) is increasing in x but current scenario of technology is updating every day, so machines are and its technologies are updating everyday but labour with the required skill is not available. Hence, for the latest technological devices this ratio is decreasing, i.e. γ_l(x)/γ_m(x) is decreasing. Labour has comparative disadvantage in updating skill to cope with new technologies.

Dis-Augmentation in Labour

We should encourage labour augmenting advancements economically as well as socially. In a technological era, automation is applied to reduce human intervention in the industrial automated world. Those who work with technology are mainly skilled people, and they had been educated with such one or more technologies. Acquisition of knowledge about advance technology provides them much professional approach and strengthen their position in their respective domains. It implicitly shows that the person must be educated with formal system in the society; but not everyone is lucky to have received primary education. One can learn professional skills by having this primary and secondary education. Many people who live below poverty line hardly educate themselves or their children. According to UN Report, 50 per cent of the world population has been deprived of the advanced technological skills.

Furthermore, labour augmenting technological advances is a time-consuming process. Migration from one technological area to another is not simple for every human being; lots of efforts need to be put in to learn advances. The migration period for a person is full of resistance as it raises issues of survival. Its psychological and social impacts are even worse as well.

According to current scenario, $\gamma_m(x)$ is continuously increasing; it is not about the number of machines that are only increasing but often inside technologies became so powerful that they produce better result with less human intervention.

Therefore, it can indirectly be considered as increase in number of machines. Besides, the demand of highly skilled people is also increasing, so the path of labour demand is now highly paid but it has also been very narrow. Hence, $\gamma_l(x)$ is decreasing, so the ratio of $\gamma_l(x)/\gamma_m(x)$ is decreasing indeed.

Ecological Changes

Overuse of automation has also reflected a number of dire consequences on nature and society. They can be divided into two different categories: first, a relationship between human and the Nature; the second, a relationship between human and society.

Relationship Between Human and the Nature

According to a report of 'Global E-waste Monitor 2020', 53.6 million metric tonnes (Mt) of electronic waste was generated worldwide in 2019. This was raised by 21 per cent in just five years. This e-waste is considered as health and environmental hazard. It contains toxic additives which damage workers as well as their children.

They can be exposed by inhaling toxic fumes through skin contact with corrosive agent and chemicals. This also leads to ingesting contaminated food and water (Forti et al., 2020: 23).

An influx of automated processes has considerably increased energy demands too. Our Nature is the only source of this energy, thus more demand of energy would consume more natural resources. Industrial development that meets the needs of present users without compromising the ability of next generation is desirable; therefore, waste of the natural resources or overwhelming use of it is dangerous for future generation. Sustainability of human has never been considered without these parameters.

Moreover, many examples of AI and robotics usages are seen in the fields of agriculture, aerospace and environment cleaning. Today's aero engineering applications like drone are used in various applications for human welfare apart from military usage. Sometimes applications of ICT are blessings as it reduces use of papers, which indirectly saves the Nature by cutting less trees. Even transportation is reduced by ICT, so this way technology favours the environment. There are some good usages of robotics in environmental sciences; it allows the monitoring and sampling of events that are dangerous or impossible for human to undertake (Dhaliwal et al., 2004).

In context of the machine operations, operators are working with the machines so their ecological system is bound with the physical work. After gaining knowledge of machine operations, tasks are transferred to the machine and operator's role is a passive one. Whenever there are combustion processes and revealing consequences of actions and we need alternatives for controlling an automated environment, knowledge of manual work is very helpful. Such operators are able to drive the control system even in critical circumstances. In the context of automation problems, loss of skills can be defined as the deterioration of manual and cognitive skills and knowledge due to the use of automatic control systems that reduce the possibility of practicing manual tasks (Anderson, 2014: 33). Loss of skills and knowledge occur as a result of operators not being able to perform the tasks manually that have been automated. This leads to deterioration of physical task performance skills. The operator's mental representation may also fade when not regularly used and maintained, thus loosing cognitive skills (Bainbridge, 1983: 775). Interesting principles have been derived for the automated system that work under the control of operator away from the manufacturing units. According to Jonas, following the principles for support system awareness raises an alarm to the autonomous system. Few are given below:

- Automate only if necessary, since automation increases complexity and complexity makes system understanding more difficult.
- Use automation as assistance for carrying out routine actions rather than higher level cognitive tasks.
- Keep the operator in control and in the loop to enhance operator abilities to detect and understand problems.
- Use methods for decision support that create system symbiosis.
- Provide control system transparency.

Relationship Between Human and Society

Use of the Internet and other electronic gadgets show that today's society is highly influenced by ICT. Poor and rich both are using this technology to control their belongings at their hands. Indeed, there have been lots of advantages of this technology during this COVID-19 pandemic when many organizations have survived successfully by using it. Many industries have faced a setback in the pandemic but IT industry galloped during this struggling period.

Due to this technology, some implicit changes are also seen directly on the human relationship. It showed possibilities that a society is dominated by individualism. The way people get along with each other is important for human relationship, but individualism breaks or stops their relationship.

The Internet

The Internet is a World Wide Web (WWW) of computers where data of computers are stored, devices are connected and therefore, users are connected to computers. In 1996, when I was first introduced to the Internet, I questioned myself how all the local networks of computers become global networks. In fact, my concerns were for security of data residing in the server interconnected through this WWW. As a student, I knew that if my computer is connected with the Internet, whole world could access it. It is difficult to identify who accessed and what data has been accessed. Research institutes and many government wings were using the Internet as a facility but it had muddled my thoughts about security of data. Gradually, I understood that it is indeed a problem and incidents like WikiLeaks confirmed that data is not secured on the Internet.

Apart from this, when you access information from the Internet, the authenticity of that data is always vulnerable. The truth is: the human managed security system faces many problems, and on the other side, digital security also has its own issues. It is not robust enough to overcome every threat that appears on this network of networks.

During the time, the Internet, being a communication interface, gained popularity and many applications used this globally available platform which grabs the attention of mass, specifically youth. There are many reasons for the popularity such as easy meeting and communicating with people, connectivity with rural as well as urban people, availability on smaller devices like mobile, palmtops, etc. even though the problems of vulnerability of data, false identity of users, fake login page for social media applications, etc. create major hurdles.

There are some ethical issues related to law; some contents are forbidden by a few countries but a server located outside the country need special treatments for violation of law. For countries having its own law system for their jurisdictions, it is possible that one thing complies with a certain country's law, but not with other countries. Similarly, from the economic point of view, monetary transactions on the Internet do need special care. For example, cryptocurrency; only a few jurisdictions have imposed restrictions on investments in cryptocurrencies, while a few like Algeria, Bolivia, Morocco, Nepal, Pakistan and Vietnam have banned some or all activities involving cryptocurrencies. Qatar and Bahrain have a slightly different approach in this issue; they bar their citizens from engaging in any kind of activities involving cryptocurrencies locally, but allow citizens to do so outside their borders. There are some countries which, while not banning their citizens from investing in cryptocurrencies, impose indirect restrictions by barring financial institutions within their borders from facilitating transactions involving cryptocurrencies; these include Bangladesh, Iran, Thailand, Lithuania, Lesotho, China, and Colombia (*Regulation of Cryptocurrency Around the World*, 2018). Hence, global policies of political, social and economic transactions need to be implemented. The biggest ethical question is: who is responsible for such a technological chaos? It is not fair to blame technology for each incorrect consequence that occurs on the Internet platform. We, as a society, need to do a lot in this regard.

Cloud Computing

A simple term for the Cloud Computing is 'centralization of data'. In the first chapter, there is a brief discussion about its technical details. Traditionally organizations were deploying hardware and software to implement various applications locally with a view to control and to transfer responsibility of data to its owner only. Being a Cloud user, control and responsibility should be shared by application owner and Cloud service providers. The services of Cloud include commissioning of hardware and software, hiring skilled manpower, maintenance and upgradation of resources. Definitely, outsourcing of required resources eases the work, but if we consider the cumulative cost of outsourcing, perhaps we will get the same return on investment (ROI) (Shah, 2014). The only advantage is: users do not have to deal with the complications of deployment, application running and maintenance. A complete offshoring of data with its storage and process implicitly imply that power is transferred into other hand.

In the essence of Cloud Computing, we find some issues relevant to an ethical analysis. First of all, the control of data shift from organizational users to the third-party services. In conventional method, data is owned and managed by organization, so responsibility is of central authority. However, Cloud makes these responsibilities segregated among many entities; these responsibilities are not in black and white form, but there are grey areas which are lacking transparencies of policies. The second issue is: storage may be segregated among various storage servers, and those are physically located across the globe. These servers are owned and managed by various organizations. Third and the most important issue is: offshoring increases the cost of data transfer to and from between the storage and users; in case of local ownership, this cost is nil.

Other ethical issues forced us to think about our conventional way of data management and processing. The question is: why to transfer control to the other platforms when conventional applications successfully serve the need of organizations? Centralization of services is also one of the issues of unemployment because it leads to the less number of people with high level of proficiency. It affects the averagely skilled and low skilled people. Another issue is: Cloud services may provide latest services but to incorporate within the organization, it would need suitable resources too. Here purpose is not to decline latest technologies but to develop compliance at local level, with cost effective solutions. For example, if a company offshored services from Cloud that is supported by 5G mobile technology, and as per today's scenario, its employees do not have such mobile handset, company has to bear the cost of handsets. Thus, ultimately cost is raised for the company. There are compatibility issues if you want to work with your current version of software when Cloud declined support to the older version.

The Internet is the backbone of Cloud technology, and we have discussed many dimensions of it in earlier section; security of data, and privacy and accessibility of data on this platform are still major issues.

Internet of Things (IoT)

The IoT involves various kinds of objects connected using wired or wireless networks. These objects are having unique addressing method for communicating each other that helps to develop a system for remotely managing devices, shops, offices and even homes. This network is used for smart cities, smart traffic control, smart transportation, etc. This system faces similar kind of problems of Cloud Computing because the Internet is the backbone in many cases. Matter of concern is physical safety and privacy.

Physical safety, in terms of IoT, means being able to reflect the behaviour of IoT devices like actuators. It is also useful to detect and prevent unintended or unexpected behaviour of control system taken on the basis of actuators. Again, we can take an incident of Arizona, driverless car accident. After the case study of this car accident, government agencies must enforce minimum standards of safety. Sometimes government is not responsible for the update of security patches released by its manufacturing agencies; user is liable to install those patches in expedient timeline. Hence, it significantly opens up another kind of ethical analysis.

There is a connection between privacy and the IoT; when IoT devices are connected with the system, it starts collecting vast amounts of user data. This data can be analysed, shared, and used for various things. We come across the fact that customers' buying habits are mined for collecting data of their personal life like pregnancy or delivery date, arrival of new baby, health issues, personal hobbies, family and kids. VA devices like 'Alexa', 'Siri', and 'Ok Google' are also generating data whenever the family is simply talking. This information is recorded, processed and stored for the future use; such phenomena raise ethical questions for the society (Allhoff and Henschke, 2018).

Conclusion

Use of ICT as a substitute for humans in various ways like human resource management in organization, medical diagnosis, vehicle driver, supplement in judicial process, etc. take the world to another level. While learning the whole system, it is revealed that certain kind of human behaviour or emotions cannot be measured by algorithms. Jobs that require human interaction and empathy covered by machine will have such robustness is a question.

AI puts four different things in front of us, for ethical use of the technology; privacy, data surveillance, bias in algorithms and human way to judge the matter. There are many debates in the world for AI should be tightly regulated but how and who should make is not there. Defined policies for the development of ICT is a demand for today because it will create severe effects in our future. European Union has already rigorous data privacy laws but still so much is needed to be done in this direction. According to Michael Sandal, 'business leaders "cannot have it both ways", refusing responsibility of AI's harmful consequences while also fighting government oversight' (Pazzanese, 2020). In the next chapter we are going of discuss about policies to meet the current need. Certainly there are many things of concern other than what we have discussed so far. Perhaps those are the roots for such a development.

Chapter 5
The Way Ahead

Currently, AI is the centre of academic agenda and public debate. This debate necessarily impacts the social lives, but its political influences are needed to be understood. There are many researches done on political impact of the AI phenomenon, yet its impacts are not clear. There is much to understand to moderate its unpleasant effects and define policies at different level.

In this chapter, we are going to see how and what matters a lot for the political phenomenon and how and who will define these polices to regulate usage of AI in various ways. Political decisions are based on social impact, and that is why government has to consider these impacts seriously. There are major impacts of AI that include global investment in technology and long-term public investment. It is stated that this has carved a new dynamic of power and logics of accumu- lation, collectively referred as surveillance capitalism (Aho and Duffield 2020). Hence, this chapter has various data and analysis of its effects by considering current phenomenon. This will disclose the real problem of the world. Latter part of the chapter contains role of four different entities – government, academia, business and individual. Their role and policies will shape the path for our tomorrow.

Real Problems

Acquiring advanced technology for our industries is not a simple matter but the need of such change is an important question for humanism. Industrial revolution had turned some countries into an economic hub with a power. It has increased an employment in the country and lifestyle of the people was improved by new gadgets. Hence, is it implied that after indus- trialization, automation will also have similar effects and society will see further upgradation. The answer to this question lies in certain facts given in the Table 5.1.

N. Shah, *Artificial Intelligence and Social Ethics*,
https://doi.org/10.1007/978-981-96-8818-0_5

Table 5.1 Effects of Industrialization and Automation

Industrialization	*Automation*
Before industrialization, there was manual work and society was mainly dependent on agriculture and its related profession	Under automation, there is complete industrialization and very little manual work
Agriculture is an unpredictable occupation; it may not return complete reward of your hard work. Nature is the factor which affects a lot in this profession, so possibility of migration is very high	Industrialization is predictable and assures you the desirable reward against hard work. But migration towards automation is not a need; sometimes people resist to adopt new automated technologies for various reasons, one of the reasons is they may be left without work
Industrialization provided employment for those who do not have work; without higher education and high skilled one can have a job	Automation is adopted in many domains (discussed earlier) and many employees were laid off and computers/robots had been placed for the work. Thus, unemployment is the one of the direct impacts. Automation required high education and high-skilled people who can deal with complex programmes

Despite the stated facts, there are certain reasons for technological development towards the automation being irresistible. In real sense, economic development is indistin- guishable from the current knowledge of technological application and its usages. One empirical study has found that nation's research and development expenditures are significant in explaining sustained growth rates over the time. Scientists and technicians involved in research and development also contribute to the creation of national technologies (Cypher 2014: 501). Table 5.2 shows recent data about number of professional researchers and the share of the total gross domestic product (GDP) devoted to R&D for various economies.

Table 5.2 Professional researchers and R&D expenditures with GDP and HDI

Professional researchers (per 10,00,000 pop.) 2015–2020		R&D expenditures (% of GDP) 2015–2020	GNI per capita (US dollars) 2018–2019
Very High Human Development (HDI > 0.905)			
France	4715	2.20	42,460
Chile	493	0.36	15,010
Korea	7980	4.81	33,790
Singapore	6803	1.94	59,590
High Human Development (HDI > 0.758)			
Brazil	888	1.26	9180
Malaysia	2397	1.44	11,230
Mexico	315	0.31	9480
China	1307	2.19	10,390
Medium Human Development (HDI > 0.64)			

(continued)

(continued)

Professional researchers (per 10,00,000 pop.) 2015–2020		R&D expenditures (% of GDP) 2015–2020	GNI per capita (US dollars) 2018–2019
India	253	0.65	2120
Thailand	1350	1.00	7260
Pakistan	336	0.24	1410
Low Human Development (HDI > 0.466)			
Guinea-Bissau	n.a	n.a	820
Nigeria	39	0.13	2030
Zambia	42	0.28	1430

Sources UNDP 2020: AnnexTableA7.1,WorldBankdatabank: https://data.worldbank.org/indicator/SP.POP.SCIE.RD.P6

According to Table 5.2, technological development of a nation is one of the important criteria to evaluate its economic growth. Countries in top order are measured with very high level of Human Development Index (HDI) and generally tend to have large number of R&D scientists and technicians. Compared to low level HDI countries, R&D expenditures of high HDI countries are also higher. Countries like Singapore are rapidly moving towards the developed country; its Gross National Income (GNI) is higher than US too. Less developed countries fall short of technology-oriented researchers, but it has been achieved by high HDI countries and already developed countries. GNI per capita is high due to high human development economics. It seems that there is a positive relationship between R&D expenditures and researchers with level of development and also in terms of income. It means that higher the technological development, higher is the HDI value. Country's technological development is the barometer of the growth. Perhaps, this is the real problem.

Changes in Policies

Threats of the AI demand changes in policies of government agencies. These changes will also reflect in other levels like academic, business and individual. Government agencies need to deal with professional researchers and technicians to investigate, prevent and mitigate malicious use of AI. Professional researchers and technicians must take the duality of nature for using such devices seriously. Besides, they also need to identify harmful applications and proactively reach out to relevant actors when it is foreseeable.

Automation seeks analysis of stakeholders about their concerns and also involves domain experts like social scientist to evolve challenges of this area like cyber crime. Laws related to malicious use of AI must be prepared with the integration of all nations in the world. Government agencies should also emphasize on following rules by business organizations and individuals. Academia also has to change their policies for the malicious use and to sustain conventional knowledge which is drained due to excess automation round the world.

Role of Government

We know that there is always a possibility of threats in digital transactions. Professional researchers and technicians under- stand this better and are aware about loopholes in the system; they can identify the frauds too; being researchers and technicians with the knowledge of domain, they can understand problems and can also apply every possible solution to prevent the malicious attacks. Government can make policies to prevent such trends.

The digital systems like mobiles, personal computers, data servers, and other devices like CCTV systems and audio system can be hacked. Users are unable to find such threats. When such private data appears in public, individual user or organization realizes about a threat. Protection of user's data should be a part of government policy and there should be pro-active threat detection system to raise alarm against the data capturing. Such alarming systems already exist; for example, when you access your Google mail account from any unknown device, system immediately sends a mail or an alert to know your concerns. Hence, extend such systems so other threats could be easily appears.

Many companies come forward with new IT policies that restrict the use of user's data collected from the social media applications like WhatsApp, Twitter, Facebook, etc. Government should investigate the access to the data and leaking holes that raises vulnerabilities of applications. Majority of users never know about the importance of their personal data; they are unaware about its use in political way or business benefits; users of the social media are accustomed to sharing their personal information and many times get trapped by antisocial elements.

In ICT there are vast updates in the software and hardware both. Many softwares come with the latest versions periodically. Such versions are having new features that uses latest technology of ICT. These versions do not last forever and after sometime, when a new version of it is released in the market, user support is also drawn back by its manufacturer. Government has two major responsibilities for such upgradation. First, decide the viability of new version and determine the clauses for the new version in the market with the latest ICT-based technology. Second, backward compatibility of the old version should not be declined. This will help society by providing guidelines for new upgradation in hardware and software when commissioning the new version. When government has control over the launching of newer versions, it can also take responsibility to map the demands with the requirements. As discussed in chapter three, two phases of innovations, the upcoming changes should be tested and its applications in the society, with the analysis of different kinds of use, should be determined by technocrats and social scientists. Hence, both government and society will be benefitted by reducing the risk of malicious use of the technology. Another benefit of this restriction is for the economy. We know that issues arise after launching the new version of the hardware or software, support to the older versions have been declined by the manufacturer. This creates hazards in many ways like compulsion to purchase new version, need to acquire new skilled workface, changes in the other related software and hardware to make it compatible with the new one. It definitely affects the economy in every way.

Few more effects of such upgradation is joblessness and/or updation of the skills of people. It is true that changes or upgradation is continuous phenomena of the ICT and joblessness in many areas is the fruit of such upgradation where high skilled people are only rescued and low skilled and middle skilled people are sufferings by losing jobs or degra- dation in scale or designation. Government involvement is required to maintain employment in every sector. I am not sure if to provide compensation to those who lose their jobs due to upgradation in technology will be helpful; because just to have compassion to survive is not a solution, giving them other appropriate work is equally important. Rehabilitation of such people should be a part of government policies.

Automation affects the ecology of the society because people become jobless due to autonomous technologies. A stakeholder analysis is necessary to find the involvement of each person in the organization and evaluate the effects of the individual and society. If changes for the automation are viable for all, then it should be applicable; otherwise, organization should resist such changes. Hence, government should decide a policy for balanced ratio of work distribution between human and machine. There should be clear provision of work trans- ferred to machine and human. Human intervention in decision-making is an important factor, so it could not only be liable on algorithms. AI and automation create usage of technology in such a way that people do not have to utilize fundamental knowledge of the domain. People who are skilled in novel technologies and use various tools should be able to work with technology; however, fundamental principles of the things are rarely known, and that create gap between domain knowledge and its application. Fundamental knowledge about domain is necessary to operate autonomous units. In a long way, this leads to higher cost of investment for any organi- zation.

Manual work has its own importance; whenever there is a failure in autonomous system, work can easily be switched over to an alternative method so that the chain of production is not disturbed. Such alternative method is manual work in many cases. Many hand-operated tasks have been converted to mechanical tasks where machine is used to develop fine products. Human operators of autonomous system are parts of our ecological system, who sustains our conventional knowledge. Thus, human work is important.

There are many different policies obeyed by different countries. One policy may contradict with the policy of another country. This is the way some persons find an easy way to deceive people and commit frauds. There should be common policies among all the nations so that there is not any gap area.

Standardization of international policies for ICT is the demand of time. Each nation should play active role in this. Government should also introduce awareness programme and start educating people about its dangers.

Role of Organization

Research organization and development organization both should be involved in policies of autonomous process. As a researcher or an organization, it is important to find duality in nature of usage for technology. If such technology is experimented in a laboratory, one can identify its malicious use or they can also provide solution to prevent such usages in the society. Moreover, they may take help of social scientists to understand nature of the society and restrict the use for malicious purposes.

Though novel innovations must be better for society, ethical values of the research should be a part of it. Dangers of technology must be disclosed by the organization so that people can learn about its ill effects. Everything introduced by such organizations should be introduced after considering their ethical and moral values for the sake of humanity.

Academia

Universities and schools are at the core of the society. These institutes should play a major role in understanding human values. In every field of academic curriculum, humanities should be an integrated part of the study. Academic institutes should incorporate this in every activity of the curriculum for the sake of the society and integrate it with the study rather discriminate as a different subject.

Laws of science have been discovered with lots of hard work and sacrifices of many scientists before it has reached to us. Their work helps us in many things which we use in our routine life. Hence, their work in form of principles of science still persist in the society through various activities done by the human. Automation will take applications of such principles in a closed system and conventional process will not directly appear in the society. Only the manufacturer knows about its functions and about its conversion into a mechanical task. Academia should play their role to preserve such knowledge and applications in the society by encouraging students to work using such principles. This will encourage the students to learn basic principles rather handover them an established autonomous system.

Advancement in a technology is not a just measure of knowledge; according to Gandhi it should be self-reliant with the help of productive economic activities like those of gardener, carpenter, mason, cobbler, etc. (Kulkarni, 2012: 138). Schools and universities need to incorporate such activ- ities in their courses which will help students to explore variety of areas where they can make their selection. Today's education emphasizes on advancement in technology without any concern for primitive needs of human and our ecosystem. Today advancement in any area is for good return of investment (RoI), but we do not convey methods for better ecosystem on the Earth. For instance, global warming is a big issue but technology has failed to provide its solution. It also increases the gap between poor and rich which needs to be reduced for a balanced society. Gandhi had suggested a new teaching way that is *nai-talim* to form a new paradigm which is worth for all above discussed problems. He said that it would give the students a perfect, well-balanced, all-round education in which the intellect, the body and the spirit have all full play and develop together in a natural, harmonious whole. Man is neither mere intellect, nor the gross animal body, nor the heart or soul alone. A proper and harmonious combination of all three is required for making of the whole man (Kulkarni, 2012: 139). Our current education system explores novel techniques to provide high comfort in human life but without considering Gandhi's vision for harmonious whole where intellect, body and heart work together.

Research Institutes

Technology is nothing but application of the laws of pure science discovered from the Nature. Scientists have discovered it for the sake of the society's benefits. When converting these laws into applications, mechanical process has been generated using various devices. These devices are working using some kind of natural energy, most of the time it is using non-reproductive energy. Converting manual processes into mechanical processes reduces the use of manpower that is reproducible.

Many times we find that illiterate people develop some instruments or procedures that help them in their daily activ- ities. These instruments are very simple; developed using local materials but such innovations never come before the society because it is used in small villages. Importance of such innovations is never less than that of the scientific innovations. Academic institutions should come forward to encourage them and introduce it as a part of students curriculums, so students should be aware and use it for other relevant solutions in the society. This way let people of the society become aware and the knowledge should spread in other communities as well. Such product or procedure is made using local material that has more potential to push up the productivity because it is developed after great experience. Most of the affected dimensions had been considered in such things. Organizations like 'Shristi' has taken initiative to bring such local innovations in the society so others (especially villages) can take advantage of it (case study of 'Shristi').

Automation of industrial machines declined the human involvement, such automation is rather degrading knowledge of human too. Universities and research institutes should not be instruments for this transformation of work because students need to learn basic principles and methods rather than relevant inbuilt technology. Technology helps when foundation of the principles is strong. Hence, it is the time to define boundaries for up to what level automation should be part of curriculum. Gradually, government will also find the reasons to restrict automation not only for joblessness but also to persist other conventional knowledge and maintain balance in the society. Let us understand this with some examples.

The role of academia is to strengthen the system by adopting a new paradigm like *nai-talim* where students can learn working with the body, heart and soul. This will not develop overnight. Once we achieve qualities of education with these three things, most of the worldly problems may get solved. Most of the academic and research organizations are researching with the latest technologies and many of them are towards automation of current process. This will lead us to centralization of power, centralization of capital and central- ization of authoritative power in use of technology.

Another thing, architects, advocates, civil engineers, etc. have organizations to develop standards for their relevant fields and ethical use of the product. Similarly, ICT should also establish an organization or committee to look into the ICT innovations and control the loopholes or violation of rules in applications with respect to humanitarian approach. Role of committee is to provide waiver after considering the ethical values and humanitarian approach of the applications (Joshi, 2021: 95).

Role of Individual

Use of technology provides strength to an individual. It makes us more independent because many things are now at our fingertips; shopping, ticket booking, hotel booking, online transactions of your payment, etc. are possible with a click. While taking an advantage of an independent life, we are losing our privacy; as a user of technology, we are sharing our personal details; we know that every operation of ours have been noted by various applications; every mode of transaction is not secure; there are chances of your data being used for other purposes without your knowledge. As a user, it is our responsibility to get aware about its pros and cons. Many articles in newspapers, many blogs, talk shows, white papers, research papers, etc. are publishing such cases. It is necessary for every literate person to update oneself and procure knowledge about such technology. One can also convey one's own experience to others about its risk factors.

Just do not rush for free products. They may ask about your personal details and/ or collect data through spear phishing or e-mail phishing. Many games on Cloud and binge-watching shows are creating psychological disorder in people (Wheeler, 2015). Many had developed suicidal tendency and killed themselves. Many such incidents were published in the newspapers. It is time to know the root cause and take actions.

An individual must know the following matters regarding online surfing and usage of AI algorithms for accurate prediction about a person's behaviour:

- Data collection from social media.
- Data collection from your mobile or e-mails called e-mail phishing.
- Data collection from your mobile GPS to know about your whereabouts.
- Data collection through some applications which use your camera.
- Details about your bank accounts through online payment.

Last but not the least, we should understand the limitation of a machine. Everything cannot be transferred to it. More ease and sophistication in life demands more alertness. We just cannot put our vital details in others' hands for the sake of ease.

Human alertness and creativity make unremarkable confidence, which is a necessity for life. Gandhi also said about the craze for machines, 'if the craze for the machinery method continue, it is highly likely that time will come when we shall be so incapacitated and weak but we shall begin to curse ourselves for having forgotten the use of the living machines given to us by God' (Jivani, 2018).

Conclusion

Looking at various effective dimensions of automation, there will be relative changes in human lives in the near future.

Many of these are in the pipeline too. No doubt, the backbone of automation is AI and that is why acquiring knowledge about it is always desirable for individuals, businesses and nations. When we talk about AI and development, it is about only economic growth. There is no humanist approach that we develop through it. Industrialization was for the limitless appetite for new sources of cheap raw materials and its market, similarly automation is the appetite for machines that decline human work on a very large scale. Market also cultivates the attraction of people by introducing novel technology of such products. It implicitly distracts us from the fraternity because self-reliance with the help of current technology provides independence of an individual, merely without collective efforts. Gandhi's idea for humanism is about the brotherhood of all living things, which is nearly impossible in the current scenario.

There are two possibilities regarding automation; one, if we take AI seriously for the so-called development, society will definitely suffer from its ill effects in near future. And if we do not, we are out of the race of development in the world. Everyone wants to sustain in this era of technology and automation that lead to the so-called development. To a certain extent it will help in survival but not always because human involvement in the automation is becoming narrow and without high skill, it is difficult to sustain. We must consider the humanistic approach towards the development and establish balance in the society.

Gandhi and Marx, on their common ground of humanism, consider such conditions as a root cause of human alienation in capitalist society. As we discussed earlier, unless 'manners' fundamentally change and our 'system' is trans- formed, mere destruction of the structural part of the society will not make any difference. Perhaps, a search for another planet to live makes sense here but demand for a society will be still the same.

Appendix A
The Impact of Automation on Employment: Just the Usual Structural Change?

Ben Vermeulen, Jan Kesselhut, Andreas Pyka and Pier Paolo Saviotti

Abstract: We study the projected impact of automation on employment in the forthcoming decade, both at the macro-level and in actual (types of) sectors. Hereto, we unite an evolutionary economic model of multisectoral structural change with labor economic theory. We thus get a comprehensive framework of how displacement of labor in sectors of application is compensated by intra- and intersectoral countervailing effects and notably mopped up by newly created, labor-intensive sectors. We use several reputable datasets with expert projections on employment in occupations affected by automation (and notably by the introduction of robotics and AI) to pinpoint which and how sectors and occupations face employment shifts. This reveals how potential job loss due to automation in "applying" sectors is counterbalanced by job creation in "making" sectors as well in complementary and quaternary, spillover sectors. Finally, we study several macro-level scenarios on employment and find that mankind is facing "the usual structural change" rather than the "end of work". We provide recommendations on policy instruments that enhance the dynamic efficiency of structural change.

Keywords: Structural change; Employment; Labor; Automation; Automatability; Occupation; Robot;Robotization; AI; Computerization

Introduction

Mankind is on the brink of the Fourth Industrial Revolution in which breakthrough technologies such as artificial intelligence, robotics, data science, quantum computing, internet-of-things, etc. will enable advanced applications such as social robots, autonomous vehicles, virtual assistants, 3D printing and desktop manufacturing, etc. (e.g., Schwab 2017). There is a debate among labor economists on the

N. Shah, *Artificial Intelligence and Social Ethics*,
https://doi.org/10.1007/978-981-96-8818-0

effects of the introduction of technology to increase productivity (or, economize on labor) in general, and of automation by means of robots and AI on employment in particular. On the one hand, there is literature arguing that the pace at which employment is destroyed by the introduction of productivity-enhancing technology may exceed the pace at which mankind is able to find new uses for those becoming unemployed (Keynes 1930). Mankind may thus face mass unemployment and increasing income inequality, which calls for unemployment relief through income redistribution and unemployment benefits (Leontief 1983). With regard to the effect of automation using robots and AI, there are articles in popular media, consulting reports (Manyika et al. 2013; Wolfgang 2016), and scientific publications (e.g., Brynjolfsson and McAfee 2011; Ford 2015; Frey and Osborne 2017) of how introduction of AI, robots, and automation affects a large share of workers and may even create a future with structurally high levels of unemployment (or even the "end of work" [Ford 2015]), stagnating median wages, and growing income inequality. With such consequences, further automation may well be economically and socially unsustainable in the long run.

On the other hand, there is a sizable body of scientific literature that argues that, although automation indeed will displace some workers, the technological change also creates demand for labor. While automation increases productivity and thereby causes unemployment, there are countervailing effects such as increasing product demand, local demand spillovers, increasing demand for new skills or even new jobs required for new products and services (e.g., Manyika et al. 2013; Acemoglu and Restrepo 2016, 2018; Acemoglu et al. 2017; Autor 2015; Autor and Salomons 2018; Graetz and Michaels 2015; Gregory et al. 2016; Stewart et al. 2015; Vivarelli 2007, 2014). Aptly phrased, Autor (2015) states: "*Automation does indeed substitute for labor—as it is typically intended to do. However, automation also complements labor, raises output in ways that lead to higher demand for labor, and interacts with adjustments in labor supply. [. . .] [J]ournalists and even expert commentators tend to overstate the extent of machine substitution for human labor and ignore the strong complementarities between automation and labor that increase productivity, raise earnings, and augment demand for labor*". Historical analysis corroborates this perspective. In the past, industrial revolutions triggered structural transformations, which, after recovering from initial technological unemployment, have brought mankind merely frictional unemployment, and prosperity rather than poverty, and it remains to be seen whether it is different this time (Mokyr et al. 2015). Thus, possibly, we are facing an economically and socially sustainable future with a high level of employment for a skilled workforce, in which the recent wave of automation is merely a period of transition with temporary technological unemployment.

In this paper, we start from the evolutionary economic notion on structural change that productivity-enhancing technology displaces labor in existing sectors yet the unemployed may be mopped up by newly created sectors (Pasinetti 1981; Saviotti and Pyka 2004, 2008). We formulate a conceptual framework of different types of sectors and occupations with regard to the temporal effects of technological change. The research aim is threefold. Firstly, to present a multisectoral perspective on the impact of automation on employment and discuss the various countervailing forces for technological unemployment within and between sectors. We thus allow for a higher degree of specificity of narratives on the structural change driven by automation and place extant labor economic theories in a sectoral perspective. Secondly, we use the assessments of occupational experts of the Bureau of Labor Statistics (BLS) to specify which actual sectors (in the North-American Industry Classification, NAICS) and actual occupation groups (in the Standard Occupational Classification, SOC) face the technology-driven employment shifts. Moreover, we use different datasets to conduct a patchwork of analyses on changes in employment based on the countervailing effects specific to the types of sectors. Thirdly, to aggregate over changes in the sectoral composition of the economy and projected employment in the various sectors, we propose several macro-level scenarios on employment in a decade from now. We isolate the actual occupations and sectors that arguably feature in the "end of work" and "structural change, as usual" scenarios and look for indications that we are in either one of the two scenarios. As we also observe that the span of occupations that are partly or entirely automatable as well as the set of sectors thus affected are limited, the "end of work" scenario manifests itself in a limited part of the economy at best. Moreover, we also argue that the loss of jobs due to automation is compensated in various ways, so ultimately we expect to merely see structural change with (possibly) a temporary dip in employment. From the labor economic effects at work, we formulate several policy measures to increase the dynamic efficiency of structural change.

In a nutshell, the empirical analysis using the multisectoral framework finds developments at odds with the "end of work" claim. For one, our expert-based estimation of the automatability of jobs in the applying sectors is counterbalanced by an increase in employment in the sectors developing, producing and supplying technology (notably engineering, software, and scientific services). Moreover, there is substantial employment growth in quaternary sectors, personal/health care, luxury goods sectors, etc., arguably due to growth in disposable income in the "making" and complementary sectors, but even for "upskilled" occupations in the applying sectors. Aggregating over changes in the sectoral composition of the economy and projected employment in the various sectors, we find support for the claim that job loss in the applying sectors is limited and outweighed by the potential for job creation in directly related (new) sectors as well as in the spillover sectors.

The structure of this paper is as follows. In Sect. "Conceptual Model", we present our conceptual framework, including our multisectoral perspective on structural change. In Sect. "Methods and Data", we discuss the data and the data-analytic methods used. In Sect. Results, we present the results of our analysis of empirical data on how (the developing capabilities of) robots and AI affect the work activities performed by humans. Moreover, we provide a brief analysis of automatability of occupations in the sector of application and present results on (structural shifts in) employment in certain technology-affected occupations in other discerned sectors. In Sect. "Conclusions, Policy Implications, and Evaluation", we evaluate our projections on how automation affects structural change in employment in the various sectors and associated groups of occupations. Finally, we propose and discuss three categories of policy instruments to prevent and overcome adverse effects of automation.

Conceptual Model

Technological Unemployment and Compensation

Automation has consequences for the organization of work, the type of jobs performed, skills required, and the tasks and working activities conducted. In general, automation (computerization, introduction of robots and AI) predominantly affects routinized work in stationary, predictable environments, typically found in the middle-skilled jobs (Wolfgang 2016; Ford 2015; Autor et al. 2003), particularly whenever tasks merely concern executing rules rather than require cognitive processing of information (Levy et al. 2007). However, automation and computerization by means of the introduction of robots, advanced software, and AI thus substitute for the routine and "rule-based" tasks, yet complement the non-routine and cognitive tasks (see, e.g., [Autor et al. 2006] on computerization). The non-routine and cognitive tasks typically are executed by high-skilled employees with high wages, while the routine tasks generally are conducted by medium-skilled employees with medium wages. Consequently, jobs that are low-skilled, but are composed of non-routinized tasks in a dynamic and unpredictable environment cannot yet be robotized or computerized. Jobs which require refined perception and physical dexterity, creative intelligence/improvisation, or social intelligence, regardless of whether they are low-skilled, are less at risk of replacement (cf.Brynjolfsson and McAfee 2011; Frey and Osborne 2017; Deming 2015). Although tasks using tacit knowledge or knowledge which is hard to codify cannot be automated (cf. Autor and Polanyi's, 2014), if there is a sufficiently large amount of data, cognitive, knowledge-based tasks can also be taken over by AI (Ford 2015) and are, as such, subject to progressive automation and substitution as well (cf.Manyika et al. 2013; Dobbs et al. 2012). Thus, technological substitution of jobs does not necessarily displace low-skilled work, but rather routinized work (Autor et al. 2003). As routinized work is often executed by medium-skilled workers, this substitution effectively "polarizes" (Autor et al. 2006; Goos and Manning 2007; Goos et al. 2009) or "hollows out' (Katz and Margo 2013) the labor force, with fiercer competition and thereby wage stagnation, particular for middle and lower skilled work.

While the introduction of productivity-enhancing technology displaces activities conducted by humans and thereby causes technological unemployment, there are various countervailing forces actually creating new activities, functions, and jobs and thus compensating for that unemployment (Acemoglu and Restrepo 2016, 2018; Acemoglu et al. 2017; Stewart et al. 2015; Vivarelli 2007, 2014). Firstly, the introduction of productivity-enhancing technology causes a decline in costs of the automated tasks. This may have firms lower their prices and thereby increase demand. This brings about an increase in demand for labor (also) in non-automated tasks. Secondly, the exploitation of the introduced technology may require complementary tasks (e.g., controlling, programming, and maintenance), which may form new occupations or new activities for existing occupations (cf. Goldin and Katz 1998; Griliches 1969). These complementary tasks may increase the demand for higher skilled employees with higher wages. Thirdly, cost savings and additional profit may well be reinvested, deepen automation, and give rise to new products and services, and thereby new jobs. Fourthly, there are local demand spillovers, such as demand for doctors, hair stylists, and waiters (Autor and Salomons 2018; Gregory et al. 2016; Moretti and Thulin 2013). There is a fifth countervailing force, namely the creation of new tasks, functions and activities in which "labor has a comparative advantage relative to machines". This causes the creation of new jobs that "reinstate" the displaced labor. Acemoglu and Restrepo (2018) argued that particularly this last effect is required for a "balanced growth path".

Multisectoral Perspective

Arguably, the labor economic process described above is driven by entrepreneurial behavior in a process of creative destruction (cf. (Schumpeter 1942)) and brings about structural change; central in the literature on structural change is the shift of demand for labor in one to other sectors (e.g.,Baumol 1967; Echevarria 1997; Ngai and Pissarides 2007). Innovation and entrepreneurial activities give rise to new products and services, which in turn may give rise to new sectors in which jobs are created. As such, over time, the sectoral composition of an economy becomes more varied and output differentiation increases (cf.Pasinetti 1981; Saviotti and Pyka 2004, 2008). Here, we propose a multisectoral perspective akin to the structural change literature as a template to study the effects of automation. We discern two dimensions: (i) the type of sector affected directly or indirectly by automation (notably: (1) sectors in which the technology is applied; (2) producing, developing, supplying and supporting ("making" sectors); (3) complementary sectors (e.g., facilitating or inhibiting exploitation of the focal technology); and (4) quaternary sectors receiving spillover); and (ii) characteristics of occupations subject to technological change (notably whether these occupations face substitution, transform to reap complementarities, or come into existence creating and reaping new technological opportunities). With the introduction of these additional dimensions, we enable providing an overview of which specific sectors and occupations are actually affected and allow further disentanglement of displacement and countervailing effects of automation.

We now revisit the labor economic framework provided in Sect. "Technological Impacts" with the multisectoral perspective as focal lens. Firstly, the introduction of productivity-enhancing technology is found to lower the net employment in the focal sector of application (cf. Rodrik 2016). However, even in the existing sectors of application, there are "intrasectoral transformations" in the forms of new, complementary tasks or even jobs created to support the use of new technology. Moreover, the negative effects of substitution might be (and actually are) compensated by increasing demand whenever products and services become more advanced (and more diverse, possibly customized) or whenever the unit costs drop. Indeed, robots and AI may well substitute and complement employment within the same sector of application at the same time (Autor et al. 2003, 2006; Goldin and Katz 1998). Secondly, with increasing automation in the sectors of application, there is an increase in demand for technological products (robots and AI) not only in the developing and producing sectors, but also in the upstream supplying and supporting sectors, which create new jobs as well (Gregory et al. 2016; Stewart et al. 2015; Vivarelli 2014; Arntz et al. 2016; Gorle and Clive 2013). Thirdly, there are jobs created in complementary sectors facilitating and inhibiting the (efficient) implementation of the focal technology (e.g., training and education), the exploitation of business opportunities (e.g., consultancy), etc. Fourthly, there is local demand spillover as disposable income is spent on discretionary goods (e.g., leisure and traveling, entertainment and culture, sports and lifestyle, etc., but also health care) and thus may increase employment in quaternary sectors (Gregory et al. 2016). The loss of jobs within a particular sector due to automation is offset by the increase in product demand and positive spillovers to other sectors (Autor and Salomons 2018; Gregory et al. 2016; Moretti and Thulin 2013). The change in total disposable income and/or hours worked is expected to correlate with the change in demand of discretionary goods. Finally, there is a sixth type of sector, which we exclude from further analysis, namely unrelated sectors, which attract employees that got displaced in the sector of application and decide to do something completely different.

Competition drives down profit margins and forces firms in existing sectors to: (i) introduce productivity-enhancing technology which displaces labor with capital; and, ultimately, (ii) look for new products and services, business models, etc., to reap "monopolistic rent" (Schumpeter 1942). As such, there is endogenous creation of new products and services which may give rise to (labor-intensive) new sectors that mop up the technologically unemployed (cf.Pasinetti 1981; Saviotti and Pyka 2004, 2008). This is in line with the labor economic notion that the creation of new products, services, functions, and activities thus reinstates displaced labor and is argued to be essential for sustained growth (cf. Acemoglu and Restrepo 2018). These new sectors generally develop or put to new use the focal technologies, or support, supply or complement (the use of) these technologies. In the long run, we expect a cascading creation of sectors developing and producing new technologies and creation of new sectors applying the developed technology, with labor mobility within and across these sectors. In addition to this, there are education and training sectors which facilitate this structural change and mobility within and across sectors.

In addition to the "type of sector" dimension, we introduce a classification of changes in occupations due to automation. We discern three classes of occupations. The first class are *existing* occupations that are directly affected by technological substitution of (part of) the tasks. This class also contains occupations that are *in*directly affected by changing demand or disposable income of customers. This holds for occupations in the sectors developing and producing the focal technology

	'Making' sectors (Producing & developing, supplying & supporting)	Applying sectors	Complementary sectors (Inhibiting & facilitating)	Spillover sectors (E.g. quaternary)
Existing occupations	+ Increase in demand for technology + Increase in demand for upstream capital goods + Deepening automation	- Displacement + Increase in demand due to lower prices due to increase of productivity	- For old technology, largely automated occupations	+ Increase in employment and disposable income in 'making' & complementary sectors - Decrease in employment and disposable income in applying & complementary sectors
Exploiting & transforming occupations		+ Exploitation of complementarities in form of new tasks or even (specialized) jobs	+ For new technology, occupations transforming and reaping complementarities	+ Increase in employment and disposable income for higher skilled workers in applying sectors
Emerging occupations	+ Entrepreneurial and innovation activities + New high skilled and high paid jobs, notably for accumulation of technological development	+ Resources freed up put to use in creating new products/ services + New applications + New occupations due to new ways of organizing, communication, new social processes, etc.	+ For new occupations and new technology	+ Increase in employment and disposable income in newly created occupations in 'making' sectors

Fig. 1 Changes in employment by type of sector and change in occupation with respect to the introduction of focal technology. The signs indicate the expected change in employment due to automation and the accompanying text the cause for the type of change. Note that some table cells report both positive and negative effects such that the net result is undetermined

or supplying products or services to robot or software builders. However, this also holds for occupations in sectors that are facilitating or inhibiting these changes, e.g., people need to be trained and educated in the new rather than old technology. Note that the net effect of technological change is not immediately obvious: while jobs in the new technology are created (e.g., trainers, consultants), jobs related to old technology may be lost. Moreover, technological change also affects the disposable income, which has ramifications for spillover into the quaternary sectors.

The second class contains: (i) occupations in which, primarily, task content is adjusted to *exploit* new technology; and (ii) occupations that *transform* substantially by introducing complementary tasks to exploit the focal technology (e.g., maintaining or programming a robot). The latter may well require a skill upgrade. Arguably, it may be that the job title stays the same but new technology is used to change the input manageable, the processes available, or the output possible, and thereby the activities required.

The third class contains emerging occupations that reap opportunities to provide innovative products or services using the focal technology, or extending and recombining technology. A substantial amount of employment growth takes place in jobs with new job titles (Acemoglu and Restrepo 2016).

Figure 1 sums up the changes in employment expected by type of sector (columns) and the type of change in occupations (rows) due to the introduction of focal technology. Although the sector of application and existing occupations face substitution and hence job destruction, the employment in all the other sectors is either growing directly due to or affected (in)directly by the emergence of the new technology.

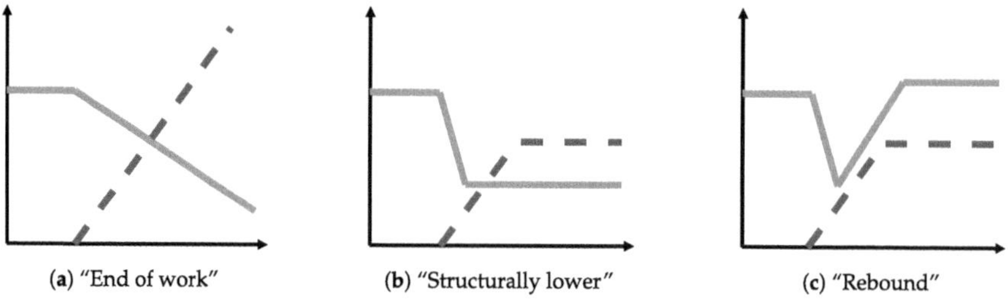

Fig. 2 Three main scenarios on the development of employment upon the introduction of robot/AI technology, with the employment share in solid lines and capital share in dashed lines. (**a**) "End of work": destroying jobs to the level of mass unemployment, (**b**) "Structurally lower": Developing a high level of unemployment, (**c**) "Rebound": After a dip, return to the previous level of employment

Macro-Economic Scenarios on Employment

With regard to the development of employment due to automation, e.g., the introduction of robotics and AI, we have to aggregate the development of the employment in the economy as a whole, across all sectors. In general, routine-replacing technical change does reduce employment (for the middle-skilled in particular), yet this is more than compensated for by increases in product demand and spillovers (Gregory et al. 2016). However, the creation of new products, functions, and activities (cf. Autor and Salomons 2018) and (thereby) creation of new sectors (Pasinetti 1981; Saviotti and Pyka 2004, 2008) may be required for a sustained and balanced growth path. It is too early for empirical studies on the *recent* generations of robots and software solutions, but there are a few empirical studies on the effects of robotics on aggregate employment in the past. Graetz and Michaels (2015) found that the introduction of (industrial) robots in several OECD countries over the years 1993–2007 did not significantly reduce number of hours worked, and, similarly, Dauth et al. (2017) found no significant effect on net employment in Germany. Acemoglu and Restrepo (2017) found industrial robots to reduce employment and wages in the United States of America over the years 1990–2007 but this is rather marginal.

From the multisectoral perspective, we know that there are two mechanism required for sustained high levels of employment: (i) labor mobility within and across sectors and possibly upskilling of labor; and (ii) creation of new products, services, etc., ultimately culminating in new sectors requiring new skills. As such, there effectively is a race between technological development with demand for particular skills and education providing people with those necessary skills (cf. Goldin and Katz 1890). With regard to the outcome of this race, we discern three scenarios (see Fig. 2).

Firstly, there is the "end of work" scenario (e.g., Ford 2015). In this case, robotics and AI will become so advanced that any job, including those created in new sectors, are soon taken over by technology again. We will end up in this scenario if the rate at which humans can be reeducated and retrained for employment is lower than the rate of technological advancement (cf. Brynjolfsson and McAfee 2011). Moreover, it requires that the job destroying potential of technology through substitution outpaces the job creating potential of technology through complementarities (cf. MacCrory et al. 2014).

Secondly, in the "structurally lower" scenario, some jobs are destroyed by technology definitively, but (a proportional part of the) displaced employees can be reeducated to find jobs in other and possibly newly created sectors. One argument in favor of this scenario is that technological advances in new sectors stifle if education cannot foresee the necessary skilled workers. As such, education in fact moderates the pace of technological progress. Note that the "structurally lower" levels of employment may also be because the number of hours worked per week may further decline.

Thirdly, in the "rebound" scenario, after a shock due to the introduction of labor-substituting technology, the level of unemployment returns to a "regular" rate of frictional unemployment (cf. (Basu et al. 2006; Trehan 2003). The rebound is driven by the countervailing effects described in Sect. "Technological Impacts" within the sector of application or within the value chain of producing and supplying sectors as well as through the creation of new sectors. Note that a structural transformation with the rise of (employment in) quaternary sectors also contributes to a rebound. Similar to the "structurally lower" scenario, education moderates the pace of technological progress, but employees can catch up faster than technology can progress.

Methods and Data

Overview

From an evolutionary economic perspective, making projections on technological developments in the future and the structural shifts in employment across the various sectors of an economy is fraught with uncertainty. Making projections is further complicated because robots, AI, and other technologies used in automation are general purpose technologies, which have a pervasive effect on a wide range of sectors and with multifaceted and (possibly) different effects within each. The impact thereof is difficult to assess because it: (i) may have opportunities revealed only ex post and advance in directions that were unforeseen ex ante, possibly spawning new sectors; (ii) require complementary investments and activities of which the economic impacts can be reaped and observed substantially later; and (iii) gradually diffuse over a range of sectors (see e.g., Bresnahan and Trajtenberg 1995; Helpman and Trajtenberg 1997).

In Sect. "Changes in Policies", we presented a conceptual model with a classification of sectors, whereby each type of sector (and its associated occupations) is affected differently by the technologies introduced in the ongoing wave of automation. Our analysis is to reveal *which* (groups of) occupations are associated with particular sectors and *how* these evolve. Generally, each type of sector requires a different approach and different data. After all, the displacement and several countervailing effects only occur in the sectors of application. Moreover, the various types of sectors compensate for the displacement of labor in the sectors of application differently. In our analysis, we focus on the types of sectors with undetermined effects (see Fig. 1) and use projections on employment for groups of occupations affected by (pending) technological change. Moreover, we are interested in detecting structural change in how demand for labor is lost in the sectors of application yet compensated for within the same or other sectors, and particularly which sectors concretely. Lacking detailed data on changes in employment in quaternary sectors due to automation, we use a long term trend in disposable income as indicator of labor demand. Moreover, occupational classifications such the SOC are conservative in adopting new occupations (job titles), such that we have to revert to using the Atlas database to get insight in groups of occupations (about) to emerge. Our analysis thus consists of a patchwork of several smaller studies.

Selection and Classification of Occupations by Type of Sector and Type of Technology-Driven Occupational Change

To be able to assess the (change in) employment in various sectors particularly with regard to technology-driven changes in occupations, we used the Bureau of Labor Statistics' (BLS) Occupational Outlook data. The BLS is an independent national agency within the Department of Labor and provides statistical data to the public, governmental bodies, business, etc. that is relevant to current social and economic issues, and accurate, impartial, and of high statistical quality. The BLS has made labor force projections since the late 1950s and, since 1968, these projections and underlying methods are retrospectively evaluated and adjusted.

We used the BLS Occupational Outlook Handbook (OOH) to selected occupations affected significantly by automation for which also employment projections (over the year 2016–2026) are available. The Occupational Utilization dataset ("Table 501") in the Employment Projections of the BLS reports the factors driving changes in employment. These factors are grouped in "productivity change", "demand change", "sourcing change", "occupational substitution", and "capital/labor substitution", but each occupation also contains a short description of occupation specific developments. From this Occupational Utilization set, we filtered occupations on keywords associated with automation, robotization, and computerization technologies (notably automa*, data, programm*, internet, robot*, comput*, technolog*, artificial intelligence, and machine learning) occur in the factor descriptions. This yielded a list of 85 occupations. On top of that, we inspected the OOH group descriptions to select occupations also affected by the focal technologies (but omitted, supposedly because of relatively strong impact of other factors), which yielded another 29 occupations.

Next, for each of the occupations on this composite list, we extracted the Industry–occupation matrix data for each of Employment Projections entries. This allows the construction of employment projections for each of the occupations by North-American Industry Classification System (NAICS) sectors (on Level 2 and Level 3). This is used to directly relate shifts in employment by occupation to changes in employment in various sectors. Moreover, using the job activity and job outlook descriptions (and notably the expected changes in these occupations), the occupations on our composite list are classified into type of sector and type of technology-driven change in occupation to fill Fig. 1. In the classification of occupations in the type of sector, we used the absolute numbers of jobs reported in the industry–occupation matrices. Whenever an occupation occurred in several types of sectors, we classified it into the type of sector with the highest number of jobs (whenever strongly asymmetric) or—in our subjective view—strongest effect of technological change. Moreover, we have used the automatability scores (see the next subsection) of occupations to classify occupations to the type of technology-driven change to the occupation. The automatability scores are suitable for that because highly automatable occupations are: (i) found in sectors in which the technology is applied; and (ii) feature a substantial number of activities which can be substituted so are "old" occupations.

Note that the OOH contains *existing* occupations. For occupations which are supposedly emerging, we turn to the Atlas of Emerging Jobs database in which occupational experts have provided descriptions of jobs they expect to see created before 2030. For examples of emerging occupations (in Atlas terms: professions), we filter the 186 occupations mentioned in the Professions Catalog on the "automatization" trend, merged with occupations which require the "programming/robotics/artificial intelligence" skill. We then select those occupations existing already before 2020. This yields 69 occupation titles. We manually assign these to a particular sector based on the occupation description.

The description and analysis of the data thus obtained are contained in Sect. "Classification of Occupations on Type of Sector and Type of Technology-Driven Change".

Scoring Occupation Automatability

The automatability assessments found in the literature generally use expert evaluation of the probability that tasks or underlying capabilities can and will be automated. Frey and Osborne (2017) looked at a selection of the O-Net occupations and assess the extent to which the main task (singular) in a given occupation has a higher than 70% chance of being automated in the forthcoming 10–20 years, which is nearly fifty percent of the jobs. After using a crosswalk table to recode the Standard Classification Code (SOC) used in Frey and Osborne (2017) into the International Standard Classification of Occupations (ISCO), Brzeski and Burk (2015) assessed the labor market in Germany and found that about 60% of jobs are at risk of being automated. Following the same approach, Bonin et al. (2013) found that, when following the approach of Frey and Osborne (2017), the number of jobs in Germany with high automatability is about 40%. Arntz et al. (2017) pointed out that focusing on occupations rather than the actual task content of jobs (which may vary from workplace to workplace) overestimates the automatability.

Manyika et al. (2017) specified for about 800 occupations, firstly, the activities (out of more than 2000) involved and, secondly, the capabilities (out of 18, divided into "input accepted", "information processing", "output delivered" and "physical movement") required for each activity based on the way humans perform them. A score the automatability of the capabilities thus translates into the automatability of the occupations. They found that only few jobs can be automated completely, but also that, for about 60% of occupations, at least one third of the activities can be automated.

Here, we assess the automatability of occupations by looking at the automatability of the underlying work activities as specified in the O-Net 22.2 database. In this database, there are four classes of work activities distinguished: (i) information input (where and how are data obtained required to perform this job?); (ii) interacting with others (what interactions with other persons or supervisory activities occur while performing this job?); (iii) mental processes (what processing, planning, problem-solving, decision-making, and innovating activities are performed with job-relevant information?); and (iv) work output (what physical activities are performed, what equipment and vehicles are operated/controlled, and what complex/technical activities are accomplished as job outputs?).

Firstly, we selected all 966 occupations in the O*Net database for which work activities have been assessed by occupational experts. Secondly, we used the O*Net-SOC crosswalk table to match the (somewhat more refined) O*Net occupational classification with the standard occupational classification (SOC) used in the BLS Occupational Outlook Handbook (OOH) dataset. We thus ended up with 702 occupations with standard occupation coding for which we have the Employment Projections over the period 2016–2026 as contained in the BLS OOH. Thirdly, we construct an expert assessment (with input from roboticists in our research consortium) of the automatability of each of these work activities by asking whether it is highly likely, possibly, or highly unlikely that a particular activity can be automated in the forthcoming 10 years. We hereby divide the work activity in three levels in which a work activity can physically or mentally challenging. Typically, very challenging activities cannot (yet) be performed by robots or AI. Based on the likelihood that a particular task for a work activity is expected to be automatable in the next decade, we assign an "automatability score": already or highly likely to be automated (score of 1), not likely/not unlikely (orange, score of 0.5), and highly unlikely (red, score of 0). The results are found in Fig. 5 in Appendix D. We thus get, for each work activity $j = 1, \ldots, 41$, an "activity automatability" score $A_j(l_j)$. This activity automatability is a function of the "level" l_j at which an activity as classified for the occupation review is complex/involved and/or an intellectual or physical challenge. Fourthly, we used the O*Net expert assessment for each occupation $n = 1, \ldots, N = 702$ of both the "level" l_{nj} (e.g., how intellectually/physically challenging is the activity?) and "importance" i_{nj} (e.g., how often does the activity occur relative to other activities, or to what extent is this activity central to the occupation?) to compute the "occupation automatability"

X_n for occupation n out of the weighed sum of "activity automatability" scores:

$$\mathrm{X}_n\colon = \frac{\sum_{j \in J} j i_{nj} A j(l_{nj})}{\sum_{j \in J} i_{nj}} \tag{1}$$

$$X_{\mathrm{n}}\colon = \frac{X_{\mathrm{n}} - \mathrm{mini}_k X_k}{\mathrm{maxi}_k X_k - \mathrm{mini}_k X_k} \tag{2}$$

Fifthly, we constructed a weighed score for each major group N of occupations, and the weighed automatability is computed as:

$$X_{\mathrm{N}}\colon = \frac{\sum_{n \in N} q_n X_n}{\sum_{n \in N} q_n} \tag{3}$$

where q_n is the BLS Employment Projection 2016 estimate of actual, current number of jobs in occupation n.

Results

Technology-Driven Structural Change in Employment in NAICS Sectors

The BLS data enable us to study the projected structural change of employment across actual sectors and to infer on the different countervailing effects at work in the various types of sectors. Following the method described in Sect. "Religion, Nature and Science", we obtained Employment Projections for all occupations affected by the focal technologies and broken down by NAICS sector. In Fig. 8 in Appendix B, we report the employment increase for these filtered occupations by major SOC group, for each of the affected sectors. A first observation is that the number of sectors as well as the number of jobs directly affected is limited. In the last two columns on the right, the projections in total number and percentage of increase in number of jobs are reported for all occupations per major group, not just the filtered occupations. A closer look at the projected shifts in employment within the same sector (vertically) and across sectors (horizontally) are in line with displacement and various countervailing effects and fully captured within our multisectoral framework of structural change.

Overall, there is a relatively small job loss (−75.3 k, about 0.0%) in occupations affected by the focal technologies, but a loss is in itself already in stark contrast with the high number of jobs expected to be created in the economy as a whole (11,519 k, about 7.4%). When looking at the projected growth in the number of jobs by major group of occupations, we see that there is almost exclusively a decline in the number jobs in Production (SOC 51) and Office and Administrative Support

(SOC 43) occupations. In Production, this is almost all due to a decrease in the Manufacturing sector (NAICS 31–33). Note that the job loss overall (−406.9 k, −4.3%) is much lower than the job loss in occupations affected by technology (−681.9 k people, −13.4%), underlining the effect of technological unemployment. In Office and Administrative Support occupations, the story is quite different: the number of administrative jobs in a wide range of sectors such as Manufacturing (NAICS 31–33), Government (NAICS 90), Education (NAICS 61), Wholesale trade (NAICS 42), Information (NAICS 51), and several others is declining, while the number of administrative jobs in Health Care (NAICS 62), Management support and services (NAICS 56), and Retail trade (NAICS 44–45) is increasing. Detailed analysis reveals that any (partially technology-driven) decrease affects mostly secretaries and office clerks across the aforementioned sectors, while the increase is due to job creation in service representatives, information and stock clerks. That said, the rate of increase in administrative jobs in the economy as a whole (0.6%) is relatively low compared to the total rate of job creation (7.4%), which may well be (partially) caused by a technology-driven productivity increase.

There also are several occupations in which there is a strong increase in the number of jobs, notably Computer and Mathematical (SOC 15), Management (SOC 11), and Architecture and Engineering (SOC 17) occupations. While the biggest increase occurs in the Professional, scientific, and technical services (NAICS 54) overall, there may be a shift of employment across occupations within this sector as well as in the Information (NAICS 51), and Finance and Insurance (NAICS 52) sectors. In these sectors, a technology-driven loss of jobs in Administrative jobs (SOC 43) seem to be offset by a gain of jobs in Computer and Mathematics related jobs (SOC 15), possibly created to reap complementarities (or where people may be hired to automate processes and thus cause technological unemployment). For example, in the Information sector (in which data is created, processed, and transferred), there is a loss of 43.5 k administrative jobs but an increase of Computer and Mathematical jobs.

When looking at the projected growth in the number of jobs by sector, the change is much in line with "classical" effects of automation, demographic developments and progressive outsourcing. There is a particularly strong employment growth in the Professional, scientific and technical services (NAICS 54 with about 331.8 k people), of which the Occupational Utilization reveals that there is an increasing demand for engineers, e.g., due to robotization and automation (SOC 17), but also the use of advanced digital and internet-connected devices, and outsourcing of security (SOC 15). Moreover, we observe a decrease in Office and Administrative Support (SOC 43) due to automation and an increase in Business Operations and Management (SOC 13, 11) due to outsourcing and purchasing training and consulting services. Health care (NAICS 62, 251.5 k) sees a rise on several occupations due to the aging population and several organizational changes such as the introduction of reception services and team-based structures to cope with that. The Administrative and management services (NAICS 56, 105 k people) sector sees an increase in employment, e.g., for customer representatives, as there is more outsourcing in other sectors. Moreover, there is substantial job loss in the Manufacturing sectors (NAICS 31–33, −751.1 k people), notably due to substitution, but also offshoring. Obviously, the job loss due to substitution is not (entirely) offset by *intra*-sectoral complementary jobs. It may, however, be (partially) compensated by the development of software, robot and AI as well as the production and servicing thereof, which reflects in the statistics for other sectors described before.

Illustratively, of the thirty fastest growing occupations reported in the BLS Employment Projections (see Fig. 9 in Appendix C), a total of seventeen occupations are directly or indirectly related to healthcare, either as healthcare practitioner (SOC 29) or support (SOC 31), personal care (SOC 39) or by providing training for healthcare (SOC 25). This, again is to be attributed to demographics and aging, but arguably also local demand spillover, which is related to disposable income. Five occupations pertain to computers and mathematics (SOC 15). Of the thirty fastest declining occupations reported, sixteen are Production-related occupations (SOC 51) such as operators, assemblers, setters, etc., and six Office and administrative occupations (SOC 43) such as computer and telephone operators, typists, data keyers, etc. In addition, in our subset of occupations (that are affected by the focal technologies), we see a confirmation of the trend that there is a decline in low- and medium-skilled jobs (such as assemblers) and growth in high-skill, high-productivity jobs (such as software engineers) (see e.g., Brynjolfsson and McAfee 2011). Surprisingly, there is an increase in medium- to low-skilled jobs for occupations such as stock clerks and order fillers, receptionists and information clerks, which appear to be automatable. Supposedly, this is, on the one hand, due to a demand-side increase and, on the other hand: (i) a low acceptance for digital services in occupations in which human contact is appreciated; (ii) yet relatively poor performance of automated services (so limited substitutability); and (iii) lowering of unit costs actually compensating automation with higher demand.

Conclusively, the occupational outlook data features structural change in line with displacement and countervailing effects discussed above, but also reveals that several countervailing effects and other factors (demographics and offshoring) may be counteracting.

Automatability of Occupations

For a socially and economically sustainable growth path, the labor displacement in the sectors of application must be counterbalanced by job creation within the same and other sectors. Following our approach described in Sect. "Computation and AI, we construct a comprehensive data set and compute automatability scores for major occupation groups as in formula in Equation (3). As the actual values of the automatability rely on the activity automatability score values, the absolute values have no particular meaning and are not reported. However, the *relative* values of course indicate relative automatability. Arguably, not only the automatability, but also the absolute number of jobs determine the actual probability that particular

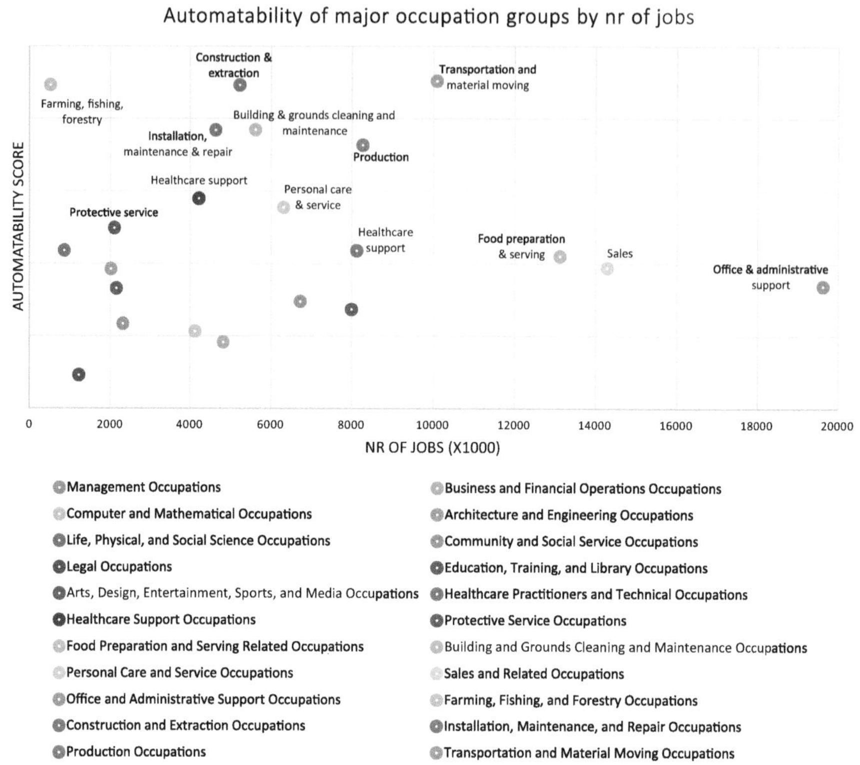

Fig. 3 Automatability of major groups of occupations, with occupations' individual automatability scores weighed by the number of jobs

occupations face automation. As such, we plot the automatability against the number of jobs in Fig. 3.

Figure 4 plots the number of jobs $\sum q_n$ for occupations $n = 1, \ldots, N$ for which the normalized automatability X^* exceeds the threshold x on the X-axis. Only 25.5% of jobs have a normalized automatability score of 0.5 (interpreted as that half of the activities of an occupation can be fully automated within 10 years). Moreover, only a relatively low percentage of 4.65% of jobs has a normalized automatability score of 0.7 or higher. Thus, in contrast to the figures reported in (Frey and Osborne 2017; Brzeski and Burk 2015; Bonin et al. 2013), we find that very few jobs are highly automatable. This is largely in line with findings in Arntz et al. (2016). Moreover, Manyika et al. (2017, see p. 5), found that, for about 60% of occupations at least one third of the activities can be automated. We find something related: just below 60% of jobs (so not occupations) has a normalized automatability of one-third or more. Thus, for roughly 60% of the jobs, roughly one third or more of all activities can be automated.

Using a straightforward translation of the automatability of work activities into automatability of the occupation, we find that the high level of automatability reported

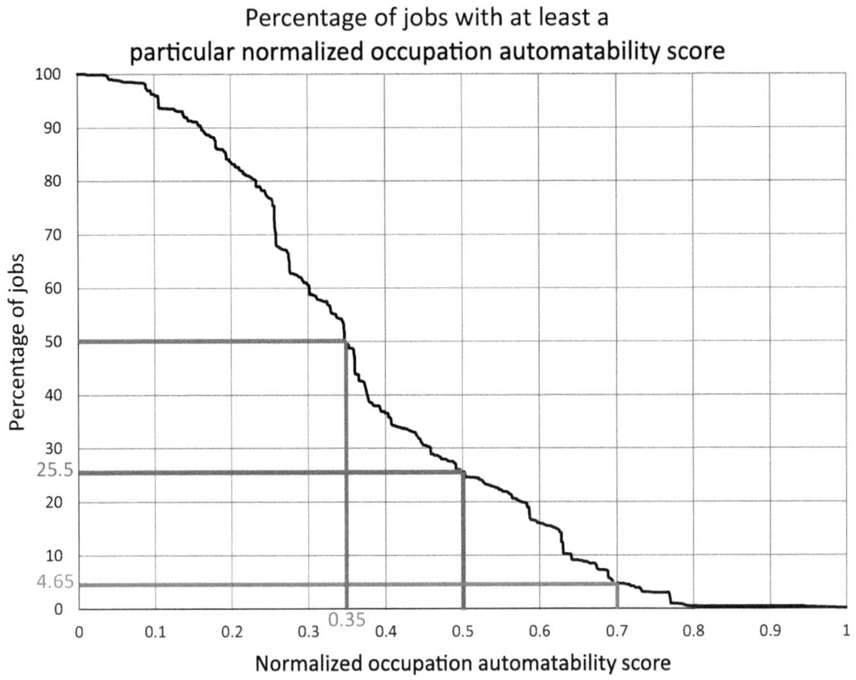

Fig. 4 The number of jobs (*Y*-axis) for occupations with a normalized automatability higher than a particular threshold (*X*-axis)

in (Frey and Osborne 2017; Brzeski and Burk 2015; Bonin et al. 2013) may well be overestimated, and actually have a much lower level such as those reported in (Arntz et al. 2016; Bonin et al. 2013; Manyika et al. 2017). In addition, neglecting the variability of tasks between workplaces also causes overestimation of automatability (Arntz et al. 2017). Thus, we have added another estimation method to the toolkit of researchers using the O*Net database (see e.g., Frey and Osborne 2017; Arntz et al. 2016), although further refinement may well be needed.

Classification of Occupations on Type of Sector and Type of Technology-Driven Change

In Sect. "Conceptual Model", Fig. 1 contains the changes in occupations subject to automation (and notably conceptions of the use of robotics and advanced software such as AI) on the one dimension and various types of sectors affected on the other dimension. As described in Sect. "Methods and Data", we have filtered the occupations in the BLS Occupational Outlook Handbook on keywords related to our focal technology. Using the job activity and job outlook descriptions (and notably the

	'Making' sectors (Producing & developing, Supplying & supporting)	Applying sectors	Complementary (Inhibiting & facilitating)	Spillover (E.g. quaternary)
Existing occupations	+ Robotics, software, electrical engineers Etc.	- Examiners, investigators, readers, data keyers - Assemblers, laborers & farm workers - Transportation & material movers - Clerks, accountants and secretaries - Machine/ equipment setters, operators, tenders - Model, die and pattern makers	+/- Teachers, trainers, educators +/- Lawyers, legal secretary work +/- Incubators, business consultants	+/- Recreation, leisure +/- Arts, culture, entertainment +/- Traveling Etc. +/- Sports, fitness, lifestyle +/- Personal care +/- Health care Etc.
Exploiting & transforming occupations		+/- Machine programmers, production system designers, installation & maintenance engineers, industrial engineers +/- Information and data handlers & collectors		
Emerging occupations	+ Robotics & software engineer in health care, agriculture, construction, education, etc. + Engineers in AI, big data, information systems, etc. Etc.	+ Operators, maintainers of new technology in health care, agriculture, information systems, construction, security, education, etc. Etc.	+ Education, legal work, consulting, etc. related to new technology	+ New media and art experiences, etc. + New recreation and leisure activities, etc. + New care services, etc. Etc.

Fig. 5 Groups of occupations by sector and type of change. The plus (minus) sign indicates there is job creation (loss) for the particular occupation, the plus/minus indicates that the development of the number of jobs is undetermined

expected changes in these occupations), the occupations are manually classified in Fig. 1. In the classification of occupations, we have used the automatability scores of occupations as a crosscheck, because highly automatable occupations are: (i) found in sectors in which the technology is applied; and (ii) feature a substantial number of activities which can be substituted so are "old" occupations with routinized, readily standardized tasks. Note that the OOH contains existing occupations. For occupations which are supposedly emerging, we filtered occupations from the Atlas database (following the method described in Sect. "Methods and Data"). These occupations are subsequently also manually classified, see Fig. 11 in Appendix E. Figure 5 contains descriptive names for aggregated groups of occupations (which are our own labels, not the SOC major or minor groups) found in Fig. 11. The color shading indicates whether employment in the occupations in particular sectors is assessed to be *decreasing* (applying sectors with existing occupations, these are subject to substitution), *balancing* different counteracting developments (e.g., complementary and spillover sectors), or *increasing* (e.g., producing and developing sectors). We now discuss the employment for each type of sector and type of technology-driven change in occupations in detail.

As expected, we see that occupations that have been classified as "substituted for" in the "applying sectors" typically are in Office and Administrative Support (SOC 43), Transportation and Material Moving (SOC 53), and Production (SOC 51) major groups which are classified as highly automatable (for a quick reference, see Fig. 3, for a detailed analysis, see Appendix D). That said, particular occupations that are economically attractive to be automated (because of both a high automatability and high number of jobs involved) according to Figure 3 do not yet show up in the OOH assessments and hence are less affected by our focal technology (i.e., automated) than expected so far. This definitely holds for Construction and extraction (SOC 47); Building and ground cleaning and maintenance (SOC 37); Installation, Maintenance and Repair (SOC 49); and Farming, fishery, and forestry (SOC 45), as well as for Food preparation and serving (SOC 35) and Sales (SOC 41). However, note that, with regard to the occupations that are at risk of being automated, our findings are largely in line with those in Frey and Osborne (2017); Manyika et al. 2017). These authors also expected Production, Construction and Extraction, Transportation and Material Moving, Office and Administrative Support, but also Sales and Maintenance and Service to be subject to computerization and robotization (see, e.g., Frey and Osborne 2017, p. 37). Manyika et al. (Manyika et al. 2017) found high automatability for the industrial sectors such as Transporting and Warehousing, Manufacturing, but also for those sectors with yet limited automation, such as Accommodation and Food Services, Agriculture, and Retail and Wholesale Trade. Note that our automatability scores and those in the aforementioned studies are based on expert evaluation of whether robots and AI can or cannot perform particular activities *within ten years*. If the automation does not materialize in the forthcoming decade, we may have to attribute this discrepancy to a technologically optimistic expert classification of what robots and software can actually do (cf. Arntz et al. 2016).

For occupations in the "making" sectors (producing and developing as well as supplying and supporting), it is not possible to determine how much growth in employment is to be attributed to automation, because of compounding of factors that affect employment (e.g., demographics, outsourcing and offshoring, technological change, and demand dynamics). As such, any figures from the BLS Employment Projections are to be interpreted prudently. As described in the Methodology Section, we made a selection of BLS SOC occupations by filtering on technology-related keywords in the factor descriptions reported in the Occupational Utilization dataset in the Employment Projections. In the descriptions of factors determining utilization, there is an increase reported for occupations headed under Computer and Mathematical Occupations (SOC 15) due to the introduction of software into devices and the use of and need to analyze more data, but also a loss due to cloud computing and offshoring as well as under Architecture and Engineering Occupations (SOC 17) due to the automation of production to cut labor costs. Looking at the OOH figures for the change in employment 2016–2026 for these filtered occupations, employment in the "making" sectors (SOC 15, 17) increases with 371.1 k jobs, while employment in the applying sectors (SOC 43, 45, 51, and 53) decreases with 464.9 k jobs.

If we include the manually selected occupations related to computers (SOC 15–11xx), engineering (SOC 17–302x), and management thereof (SOC 11–30xx) in the figure for the "making" sectors, the earlier figure changes to an increase with 659.2 k jobs. Given that the effect of the introduction of robotics and AI (taking only these "applying" and "making" types of sectors) changes from a net loss to a net gain, a detailed analysis is required for further conclusions.

Thus, already in the descriptions of factors causing an increase in projected employment for *existing* occupations, there is mention of data collection and analysis as well as development and implementation of advanced information as well as production and logistics systems. However, for *emerging* occupations, projections for employment are fraught with uncertainty. The jobs that are typically reported to be created in the nearby future are in the IT sector (e.g., in Big Data, AI, IoT, sensor technology, and general software engineering) and industrial sectors (e.g., in the automotive and robotics sector, advanced transportation and warehousing, and 3D printing) (cf. Frey et al. 2016). The Atlas database refers to more specific occupations, typically concerned with developing, producing, or applying robots, information systems, software, etc. to specific sectors (e.g., agriculture, health care, construction). In addition, consulting companies gradually start to distinguish robots (e.g., industrial versus service robots) and AI software (e.g., vision or language processing, planning, expert systems and knowledge management) on the basis of (field of) application. This underlines the progressive diversification and institutionalization central to the structural change literature.

Spillover and Disposable Income

In our multisectoral perspective, an important countervailing effect is local demand spillover (Autor and Salomons 2018; Gregory et al. 2016; Moretti and Thulin 2013), which is closely related to disposable income. Arguably, people spend their disposable income (to a certain extent) in what we consider the quaternary sectors, i.e., leisure and traveling; arts, theater and culture; sports and lifestyle; books and magazines; entertainment sectors making music, series, film and computer games; gambling; etc. As such, the employment in these "spillover" sectors evolves with the total disposable income made in the sectors in which our focal technologies are applied, developed and produced, supplied and supported as well as in the complementary sectors (e.g., education, legal support, and business consulting). Taking the BLS occupation group SOC 27 as an indicator of the employment in the quaternary spillover sectors, we see that the BLS OOH reports an estimated growth of 2158.5 k to 2276.2 k jobs over the years 2016–2026, which, with a growth rate of 5.5% over 10 years, actually has a lower than the estimated average growth rate of the employment in the economy as a whole, which is 7.3%. Arguably, we are considerably underestimating the spillover effect, because people also spend their disposable income on personal and health care service, both more luxurious consumable and durable goods, etc., all accounted for in figures of other sectors. If we consider health and personal care also a spillover category and account for change in the occupation groups SOC 29, 31, and 39, the rate of growth over the years 2016–2026 is a much higher 17.3%, outweighing the average employment growth rate.

Table 1 reports the development of the (projected) disposable income over the years 1996–2026. Note that the disposable income increased even during the financial crisis. Moreover, we observe that the increase in employment in the spillover sectors is lower than the increase in disposable income. As argued, part of the income may be spent on more luxurious consumables and durable goods (or saved, possibly effectively deferring consumption to the future). That said, with a continued growth in disposable income, we also expected an increase in employment in the quaternary

Table 1 Disposable income and the rate of change (in percentages over 10 years and annually) over the years 1996–2026 in the U.S.A

	1996	2006	2016	2026	RoC 96–06	RoC 06–16	RoC 16–26
Disposable personal income	5829.9	10,036.9	13,968.6	21,178.2	72.2% (5.6%)	39.2% (3.4%)	51.6% (4.2%)
Disposable personal income, chained 2009 dollars	7476.1	10,595.5	12,608.7	15,440.4	41.7% (3.5%)	19.0% (1.8%)	22.5% (2.0%)
Per capita disposable income	21,607.6	33,598.2	43,182.6	60,506.5	55.5% (4.5%)	28.5% (2.5%)	40.1% (3.4%)
Per capita disposable income, chained 2009 dollars	27,708.6	35,467.9	39,160.4	44,112.9	28.0% (2.5%)	10.4% (1.0%)	12.6% (1.2%)

sector. The development of disposable income for occupations differs for the various types of sectors. In a nutshell, we expect that, in the sector of application, there is pressure on the wages (and thereby disposable income) in occupations facing substitution, but not if tasks are added that require upskilling. Similarly, disposable income in facilitating and inhibiting sectors is expected to decrease (increase) for occupations related to old (new) technology. Finally, the wages and thereby disposable incomes in the "making" sectors are expected to increase.

Macro-Level Development of Employment: A Structural Rebound?

In Sect. "Technology Crisis", we report three basic scenarios on the macro-economic development of employment. Empirical evidence in Basu et al. (2006) and Trehan (2003) indicates that a short-run dip in employment is followed by a bounce back to "regular" levels of (frictional) unemployment. This is corroborated by the long run employment levels, see for instance the levels reported for the UK by the Bank of England in Appendix A. Empirical evidence shows that the unemployment rate, although fluctuating, remains fairly stationary for a century and a half, effectively absorbing major sectoral shifts, a rapid increase of women's and migrant workers" participation on the labor market (see Fig. 6). That said, at the same time, the hours worked annually decreased substantially in OECD countries (see Fig. 7), effectively countering an increasing in unemployment otherwise observed (see Appendix A).

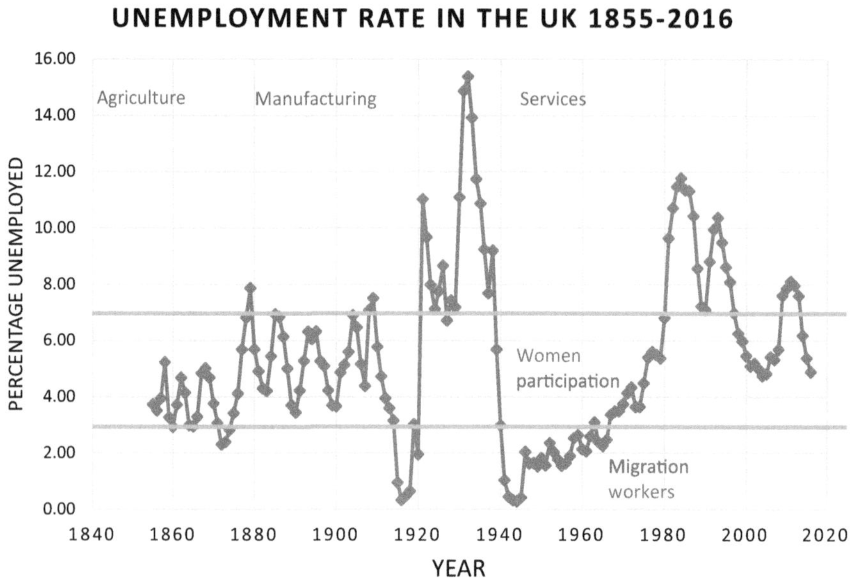

Fig. 6 Unemployment in UK over the last century and a half with labels for significant labor market changes. Data source: Bank of England, "Millennium of Data" dataset. Own visualization

A critical remark is, hence, that the atomistic view on single jobs as employment measure is somewhat misleading; there may be covert technological unemployment. Note that the drop in the number of working hours reduces disposable income, yet frees up time to spend that disposable income, e.g., on products and services provided by quaternary sectors.

Our preceding analysis reveals that the span of occupations that are partly or entirely automatable as well as the set of sectors thus affected by automation are limited. Consequently, the "end of work" scenario manifests itself in a limited part of the economy at best. We also argued that the loss of jobs due to automation is compensated in various ways. We found that an increase in employment in the "making" as well as "applying" sectors is projected, which includes new occupations related to data, advanced information and production systems, advanced applications of software, etc. The rapid rates of growth of jobs in these occupations may well be able to compensate for the destroyed jobs in "old" occupations (particularly those facing substitution). On top of that, we have observed a strong increase in disposable income which is expected to sustain the high growth rates in employment in quaternary sectors and personal care and healthcare sectors.

Thus, on top of the fact that the number of sectors affected by automation is limited, we have (mostly qualitative) observations that job loss in the applying sectors is limited. This may be well counterbalanced by job creation both in directly related (new) sectors as well as in the spillover sectors. As such, we expect that, if we see a dip in employment in the forthcoming years, this will merely be temporary

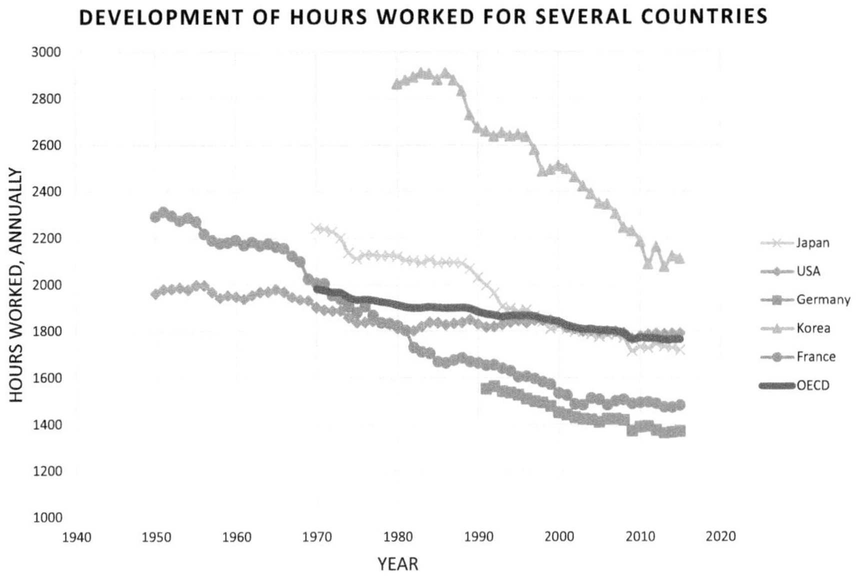

Fig. 7 Hours worked over the last couple of decades for several OECD countries. Data source: OECD. Own visualization

and in a limited set of sectors, and that, ultimately, there is a rebound to frictional unemployment levels. In the next section, we provide recommendations on policy measures that enhance inter-occupational and geographical mobility and thus assist in such a rebound.

Conclusions, Policy Implications, and Evaluation

Conclusions

In this paper, we build upon evolutionary economic notions of structural change to provide a conceptual framework on the effects of automation on types of sectors and developments of occupations, over time. We positioned the displacement and countervailing effects found in recent labor economic literature within this framework. We thus allow for a higher degree of specificity of narratives on the structural change driven by automation and place extant labor economic theories in a sectoral perspective. We subsequently used expert assessments on projections of employment in various (groups of) occupations in the forthcoming decade to study the foreseen changes in employment within and across the various types of sectors we discerned. The multisectoral perspective also highlighted how a detailed empirical analysis requires a patchwork of analyses specific to the type of sector. For the sectors of application, a study of automatability of jobs and the various intra- and intersector compensations is required. For the quaternary spillover sectors, a study of disposable income in both the making, applying, and complementary sectors is required. The supplying and complementary sectors are to be studied in conjunction with the producing and developing sectors. Such specific analyses are required not only for the projected employment as we did here, but arguably also for the development of wages, the occupational profile, etc.

We subsequently also used this conceptual model to conduct empirical analysis to provide projections which are found to be at odds with the "end of work" claim. For one, our expert-based estimation of the automatability of jobs in the applying sectors showed to be limited and the shifts of employment to the "making" sectors (notably engineering, software, and scientific services) salient. We revealed that there is substantial job creation in "making" sectors as well as in complementary facilitating and inhibiting sectors both in existing and emerging occupations. In addition, we provided an array of occupations mentioned as job creators of the future (e.g., big data and information systems, service robots, and an array of applications thereof). Moreover, we saw that growth in quaternary sectors, and possibly personal/health care, luxury goods sectors, etc. are growing faster than the average growth in disposable income, which we expect to remain high in the "making" and complementary sectors, but even for upskilled occupations in the applying sectors.

Aggregating over changes in the sectoral composition of the economy and projected employment in the various sectors, we found support for the "rebound" scenario: the job loss in the applying sectors is limited, while the potential for job creation is substantial, both in directly related (new) sectors as well as in the spillover sectors. Arguably, the "end of work" literature and notably the articles in popular media may be focused too much on loss of jobs in sectors of application and thus overlook the generation of jobs in the developing and producing (e.g., robotics technology) and supplying and supporting sectors (e.g., component producers), but also disregard the complementary facilitating and inhibiting sectors (e.g., education) and quaternary sectors receiving spillovers (sectors such as leisure and traveling, sport and lifestyle, entertainment, arts and culture). Thus, rather than the "end of work" within the set of "technology affected" sectors, we find support for "the usual structural change".

Policy Implications

As a final contribution, we discuss three types of policy interventions that have been proposed both in popular media by captains of industry and by scholars in political economic literature. Firstly, policies may regulate the introduction of robotics and AI by blocking, regulating, or taxing the implementation, to thus curb the adoption. Bill Gates, for one, advocated introducing a "robot tax", also to help out those that got unemployed due to automation, computerization, and robotization. However,

Gasteiger and Prettner (2017) shows that robot tax may merely increase the equilibrium wage rate but does not structurally change the outcome. Moreover, as "robot tax" may drive capital abroad, such regulations are best implemented internationally.

Secondly, policies may seek to "counter the adverse effects" of substitution such as income disparity. Some advocate the implementation of a system to redistribute income. Elon Musk and Richard Branson, to name a few, argue that robotization and the introduction of AI are likely to put millions of people out of a (sufficiently paid) job and call for a system of wealth distribution such as the "universal basic income". While such an unconditional income may buffer against poverty and guarantee access to resources required for sustaining particular living conditions (Colombino 2015; Parijs 1995), there are open issues on the sourcing, costs, and effects (e.g., growth, inflation rates, and participation).

Thirdly, and this is one we propose from our evolutionary economic perspective on multisectoral structural change, to "enhance dynamic efficiency of the structural transition". This is done by an array of measures such as ironing out friction–technological unemployment, stimulating the creation of new ventures, and ensuring inclusion of the (low-skilled) unemployed by facilitating/stimulating upgrading skills. Rather than inhibiting substitution in the sectors being automated and rather than merely alleviating those being replaced, the structural transition of the economy could be assisted and facilitated by educating the employees being substituted in the existing sectors to find a job in the new sectors emerging. The European Commission (see 2007) argues that an integrated mix of policy measures is required to close existing skill gaps. Central in this is that those that are unemployed receive adequate training to facilitate sustainable, upward mobility. To this end, policy measures are to ensure that employees are upskilled (within the sector of application) and receive training for new skills (also within new sectors) at the rate at which they are laid off due to substitution (cf. Goldin and Katz 1890). In addition, contractual arrangements are to be put in place to entice and encourage employers to hire low-skilled employees. Moreover, countries may seek to enhance their education system to develop a labor force working in jobs in which computers, robots, and AI are complements rather than substitutes. To further enhance the dynamic efficiency of the structural transition, entrepreneurial initiatives should be encouraged as this will enhance the creation and exploitation of opportunities in existing sectors and (formation of) new sectors. A study commissioned by the European Commission revealed a similar insight and, in addition, shows that there are substantial opportunities for entrepreneurs (Forge and Blackman 2010). Ultimately, there may be synergistic mix of these policy measures. After all, dynamic efficiency of a structural transition may be enhanced by the universal basic income as this provides people with the opportunity to pursue entrepreneurship (which contributes directly and indirectly to employment), unleashes creativity of which the benefits accrue to the quaternary sectors but also the innovativeness of traditional sectors, etc. In addition, taxation of automation technology may dampen the (bursty) rate of substitution and provide educational institutes to keep pace in reskilling the unemployed. Further research into the effects of these policy measures is required.

Evaluation

Any forecast or projection of employment is based on particular (speculatively) assumptions in the model (cognitive, mathematical, etc.) of the future, and the quality of the input data extrapolated. Conclusions based on the BLS projections implicitly derive from the model assumptions and the limitations of instruments to acquire that input data. We discuss three issues with regard to our conclusions on the nature and magnitude of change in employment.

Firstly, many new products, services, occupations, and sectors related to technologies such as robots and AI have yet to emerge, which is likely to cause an underestimation of future employment. After all, the BLS Occupational Outlook uses the job counts, wage estimates, etc. in the Standard Employment Matrix for its projections. However, the occupational classification system therein is only extended ex post and thus omits counting jobs in emerging occupations not contained in the SOC yet. Recall that we resorted to using the Atlas database for illustrations of (types of) emerging occupations. Similarly, both the NAICS and the BLS' own sector plan as well as the input–output matrix used in the estimation of demand for particular occupations are extended conservatively. The BLS currently does not provide projections on the labor demand, wages, etc. in emerging sectors, nor computes the consequences of/for these new sectors through input–output analysis. Consequently, the actual demand for labor and wages may well be higher.

Secondly, ideally, we would provide statistical support for the rates of employment change in the various types of sectors and the entire economy. However, the level of aggregation of sectors in the BLS employment projections, the polytypic nature of some of the sectors (e.g., may be "applying" as well as "making"), the lack of measures/proxies for the (possibly still moderate) magnitude of substitution and countervailing effects as well as other, general factors (e.g., demographics and offshoring), etc. all inhibit arriving at a refined multisectoral (regression) model of employment change. Moreover, arguably, we should study, in conjunction, the height and development of wages to provide projections on the rate of adoption of labor saving capital and thereby employment effects. In addition, to study the atypical countervailing effect of demand spillovers, we need measures/proxies for the disposable income in the "regular" sectors (making, applying, and facilitating/inhibiting) as well as consumption patterns. A further complication is that sectors (and occupations) that have yet to emerge can only be modeled abstractly.

Thirdly, the BLS derives its detailed projections at the occupation and sector level from the aggregate level of employment through the input–output structure and the employment matrix. The aggregate level of employment thus functions as a moderating variable. The BLS assumes that the total employment converges to the non-accelerating inflation rate of unemployment (NAIRU) over the horizon of the projections (here: during the period from 2016 to 2026). This level itself is a projection of the level of techno-frictional unemployment in the future, which in essence also reflects experts' assessment of the consequences of automation. Consequently, whether or not the entire economy sees the "end of work" is an implicit assumption.

However, note that the "end of work" in our case is defined as sustained unemployment in our focal set of making, applying, facilitating/inhibiting, and spillover sectors (including newly created sectors), which is only the case if there is no migration of these unemployed to sectors not contained in our set. To put matters in perspective: according to the sector information extracted from BLS' industry–occupation matrix, the technology-affected occupations contained in the making and applying sectors is—roughly—at most 20% of the jobs.

To overcome several of these limitations, make different model assumptions, and cater to our specific research needs, we plan to develop a detailed, evolutionary model extending our prior work (Saviotti and Pyka 2004, 2008). In this model, we seek to integrate the various labor economic effects, wages (and disposable income), endogenous rates of capital substitution, and control for exogenous factors such as demographics and international competition.

Author Contributions: B.V. wrote the final document. J.K.provided drafts for several paragraphs in the Methodological as well as the Data Analysis Sections. All co-authors proofread and commented on (earlier) versions of the text. B.V. and J.K. collected, processed, analysed, and interpreted the data as well as developed the methodological approach. P.S., A.P., and J.K. provided B.V. with additional literature and advice on positioning. B.V. formulated the (conceptual) multisectoral perspective (building upon talks on structural change with P.S. and A.P.), the macro-level development scenarios, formulated the research questions, drew conclusions, and conceived the policy interventions.

Acknowledgements: Ben Vermeulen and Andreas Pyka gratefully acknowledge EU H2020 funding for the REELER project (grant 731726) aiming to provide a policy road map addressing societal concerns on the implementation and diffusion of robotics. We thank Mirheta Omeroviv for research assistance in an early stage.

Conflicts of Interest: The authors declare no conflict of interest.

Appendix B. Employment Projections by SOC Major Groups of Technology-Affected Occupation by NAICS Sector

See Fig 8.

	NAICS sector	540000 Professional, scientific, and technical services	620000 Healthcare and social assistance	560000 Administrative and support and waste management and reme	44-450 Retail trade	48-490 Transportation and warehousing	510000 Information	230000 Construction	520000 Finance and insurance	550000 Management of companies and enterprises	210000 Mining, quarrying, and oil and gas extraction	710000 Arts, entertainment, and recreation	110000 Agriculture, forestry, fishing and hunting	220000 Utilities	720000 Accommodation and food services	530000 Real estate and rental and leasing	810000 Other services (except public administration)	610000 Educational services; state, local, and private	420000 Wholesale trade	900000 Government	31-330 Manufacturing	TOTAL Total nr change for technology-affected occupations	Total nr of jobs in technology affected occupations	Percentage for technology-affected occupations	TOTAL Total nr change for whole economy 2016 - 2026	Percentage for whole economy 2016 - 2026
11-0000	Management Occupations	31.5	64.4	4.0	5.7	1.1	8.4	1.0	8.9	7.1	0.6	0.3	0.0	0.2	0.3	0.6	0.8	3.4	5.1	2.2	-6.2	139.4	1275.9	10.9	807.3	8.5
13-0000	Business and Financial Operations Occupations	26.1	12.8	11.8	0.0	1.8	1.3	1.6	-0.6	3.9	0.6	0.4	-0.2	-0.2	0.5	0.5	1.3	2.5	-3.3	-7.5	-14.7	38.6	1692.2	2.3	773.8	9.6
15-0000	Computer and Mathematical Occupations	201.9	5.6	9.5	2.8	0.8	66.0	0.3	31.6	11.7	0.4	0.1	0.0	0.2	0.0	0.5	1.5	7.2	2.1	6.1	-6.1	342.2	1876.5	18.2	607.5	13.7
17-0000	Architecture and Engineering Occupations	88.6	0.3	4.7	0.1	1.0	-1.2	7.1	0.1	4.3	1.6	0.0	0.0	1.9	0.0	0.0	0.5	1.2	2.5	2.7	4.2	119.6	1760.4	6.8	194.3	7.5
19-0000	Life, Physical, and Social Science Occupations	0.6	0.0	0.0	0.0	0.0	0.0	0.0	0.0	0.0	0.0	0.0	0.0	0.0	0.0	0.0	0.1	0.0	0.0	0.2	0.0	0.9	35.9	2.5	124.8	9.6
21-0000	Community and Social Service Occupations	0.0	0.0	0.0	0.0	0.0	0.0	0.0	0.0	0.0	0.0	0.0	0.0	0.0	0.0	0.0	0.0	0.0	0.0	0.0	0.0	0.0	0.0	0.0	371.9	14.5
23-0000	Legal Occupations	0.0	0.0	0.0	0.0	0.0	0.0	0.0	0.0	0.0	0.0	0.0	0.0	0.0	0.0	0.0	0.0	0.0	0.0	0.0	0.0	0.0	0.0	0.0	116.2	9.1
25-0000	Education, Training, and Library Occupations	0.0	0.0	0.0	0.0	0.0	0.0	0.0	0.0	0.0	0.0	0.0	0.0	0.0	0.0	0.0	0.0	0.0	0.0	0.0	0.0	0.0	0.0	0.0	888.9	9.4
27-0000	Arts, Design, Entertainment, Sports, and Media O	-0.3	0.0	0.0	0.0	0.0	1.4	0.0	0.0	0.0	0.0	0.1	0.0	0.0	0.0	0.0	0.0	0.0	0.0	0.0	0.0	1.2	25.1	4.8	168.1	6.1
29-0000	Healthcare Practitioners and Technical Occupatio	2.6	20.5	2.3	0.2	0.0	0.1	0.0	0.7	0.6	0.0	0.0	0.0	0.0	0.0	0.0	0.0	0.4	-0.1	0.3	0.0	27.6	206.3	13.4	1336.6	15.3
31-0000	Healthcare Support Occupations	0.0	0.0	0.0	0.0	0.0	0.0	0.0	0.0	0.0	0.0	0.0	0.0	0.0	0.0	0.0	0.0	0.0	0.0	0.0	0.0	0.0	0.0	0.0	1019.6	23.6
33-0000	Protective Service Occupations	0.0	0.0	-0.1	0.0	0.0	0.0	0.0	0.0	0.0	0.0	0.0	0.0	0.0	0.0	0.0	0.0	-0.6	0.0	-2.6	0.0	-3.3	9.4	-35.1	158.2	4.5
35-0000	Food Preparation and Serving Related Occupatio	0.0	0.0	0.0	0.0	0.0	0.0	0.0	0.0	0.0	0.0	0.0	0.0	0.0	0.0	0.0	0.0	0.0	0.0	0.0	0.0	0.0	0.0	0.0	1232.0	9.3
37-0000	Building and Grounds Cleaning and Maintenance	0.0	0.0	0.0	0.0	0.0	0.0	0.0	0.0	0.0	0.0	0.0	0.0	0.0	0.0	0.0	0.0	0.0	0.0	0.0	0.0	0.0	0.0	0.0	523.8	9.3
39-0000	Personal Care and Service Occupations	0.0	0.0	0.0	0.0	0.0	0.0	0.0	0.0	0.0	0.0	0.0	0.0	0.0	0.0	0.0	0.0	0.0	0.0	0.0	0.0	0.0	0.0	0.0	1227.6	19.1
41-0000	Sales and Related Occupations	3.6	0.0	0.2	0.1	0.0	0.2	0.1	0.0	0.2	0.0	0.0	0.0	0.0	0.0	0.0	0.0	0.0	1.4	0.0	-0.6	5.2	74.9	6.9	458.7	2.9
43-0000	Office and Administrative Support Occupations	-27.9	152.0	64.5	63.4	0.8	-43.5	9.6	-15.3	-19.1	1.6	-0.9	-4.0	-5.6	-6.6	-20.3	-38.8	-59.0	-51.6	-74.3	-82.0	-157.0	15548.5	-1.0	149.6	0.6
45-0000	Farming, Fishing, and Forestry Occupations	0.1	0.1	0.1	-0.1	0.0	0.0	0.0	0.0	0.0	0.0	0.1	-0.1	0.0	0.1	0.0	0.0	0.1	-1.6	-0.3	-0.9	-2.4	325.3	-0.7	-3.5	-0.3
47-0000	Construction and Extraction Occupations	0.0	0.0	0.0	0.0	0.0	0.0	0.0	0.0	0.0	0.0	0.0	0.0	0.0	0.0	0.0	0.0	0.0	0.0	0.0	0.0	0.0	0.0	0.0	747.6	11.0
49-0000	Installation, Maintenance, and Repair Occupatio	0.6	0.0	1.1	0.2	0.9	-0.2	4.3	0.0	0.1	2.2	0.0	0.0	0.2	0.0	0.6	6.7	0.1	1.7	1.0	12.0	31.5	476.1	6.6	388.2	6.6
51-0000	Production Occupations	2.6	-5.3	-3.5	1.7	1.7	-1.7	-0.2	0.0	-0.3	0.6	-0.1	0.0	-0.5	-0.1	-0.4	-1.9	-0.2	-22.1	0.0	-652.2	-681.9	5080.0	-13.4	-406.9	-4.3
53-0000	Transportation and Material Moving Occupations	1.8	1.1	10.4	6.0	22.9	-0.3	4.5	0.0	0.5	0.9	1.0	0.6	0.0	0.1	1.0	7.4	0.6	7.9	1.3	-4.6	63.1	1008.3	6.3	634.3	6.2
	TOTAL	331.8	251.5	105.0	80.1	31.0	30.5	28.3	25.4	9.0	8.5	1.0	-3.7	-3.8	-5.7	-17.5	-22.4	-44.3	-58.0	-70.9	-751.1	-75.3	29394.8	-0.3	11518.6	7.4

Fig. 8 BLS Employment Projections for all occupations affected by our focal technologies, here grouped by SOC major groups and broken down to NAICS sectors. The absolute number of jobs for all occupations, the share of employment of occupations affected, and the number and percentage of change in employment are also reported for the SOC major groups

Appendix C. Fastest Growing and Declining Occupations, Projection 2016–2026

See Fig. 9.

Appendix D. Automatability Scores for Work Activities

Figure 10 contains color coded scores for automatability of work activities. This is based on an expert assessment of the probability that particular activities can be automated in the forthcoming decade, which coded is in three values: already or highly likely that it can be automated (regular font, score of 1), not likely/not unlikely (cursive font, score of 0.5), and highly unlikely (bold font, score of 0). The examples mentioned in the cells are provided by O*Net and are merely illustrative for three levels of complexity and intellectual/physical challenges in tasks for the work activities at hand.

Appendix E. Classification of Technology-Affected Occupations

After filtering the BLS OOH occupations based on keywords indicating that these occupations are affected by our focal technologies, the occupations have been classified to sector type and type of change of the occupation. These occupations are contained in the "existing" and "transforming" occupations rows in Figure 11. Atlas database occupations flagged as engaged in "automatization" or requiring "programming/robotics/artificial intelligence" skills are contained in the "emerging" occupations row. A plus (minus) sign indicates the occupation faces job creation (destruction), a plus-minus sign indicates opposite effects are at work and the net results is undetermined.

Major occupation group	Occupation	SOC	Proj. nr	Proj. rate
Construction and extraction	Solar photovoltaic installers	47-2231	11.8	104.9
Installation, maintenance & repair	Wind turbine service technicians	49-9081	5.6	96.3
Healthcare support	Home health aides	31-1011	431.2	47.3
Personal care and service	Personal care aides	39-9021	777.6	38.6
Healthcare practitioners	Physician assistants	29-1071	39.6	37.3
Healthcare practitioners	Nurse practitioners	29-1171	56.1	36.1
Computer and mathematical occupa	Statisticians	15-2041	12.6	33.8
Healthcare support	Physical therapist assistants	31-2021	27.4	31.0
Computer and mathematical occupa	Software developers, applications	15-1132	255.4	30.7
Computer and mathematical occupa	Mathematicians	15-2021	0.9	29.7
Healthcare support	Physical therapist aides	31-2022	15.3	29.4
Installation, maintenance & repair	Bicycle repairers	49-3091	3.6	29.3
Healthcare support	Medical assistants	31-9092	183.9	29.0
Healthcare practitioners	Genetic counselors	29-9092	0.9	29.0
Healthcare support	Occupational therapy assistants	31-2011	11.4	28.9
Computer and mathematical occupa	Information security analysts	15-1122	28.5	28.5
Healthcare practitioners	Physical therapists	29-1123	67.1	28.0
Computer and mathematical occupa	Operations research analysts	15-2031	31.3	27.4
Protective services	Forest fire inspectors and prevention s	33-2022	0.5	26.6
Healthcare support	Massage therapists	31-9011	42.1	26.3
Education and training (here: health r	Health specialties teachers, postsec	25-1071	60.6	25.9
Construction and extraction	Derrick operators, oil and gas	47-5011	2.8	25.7
Construction and extraction	Roustabouts, oil and gas	47-5071	12.4	24.8
Healthcare support	Occupational therapy aides	31-2012	1.8	24.7
Healthcare support	Phlebotomists	31-9097	30.1	24.5
Personal care and service	Nonfarm animal caretakers	39-2021	58.5	24.2
Construction and extraction	Rotary drill operators, oil and gas	47-5012	4.0	24.2
Education and training (here: health r	Nursing instructors and teachers, pos	25-1072	16.3	24.0
Healthcare practitioners	Occupational therapists	29-1122	31.0	23.8
Construction and extraction	Service unit operators, oil, gas, and m	47-5013	9.7	23.4

Major occupation group	Occupation	SOC	Proj. nr	Proj. rate
Transportation and material moving	Locomotive firers	53-4012	-0.9	-78.6
Healthcare practitioners	Respiratory therapy technicians	29-2054	-6.1	-56.3
Protective service occupations	Parking enforcement workers	33-3041	-3.3	-35.3
Office and administrative support	Word processors and typists	43-9022	-24.8	-33.1
Installation, maintenance & repair	Watch repairers	49-9064	-0.5	-29.7
Installation, maintenance & repair	Electronic equipment installers and r	49-2096	-3.1	-25.6
Production	Foundry mold and coremakers	51-4071	-3.0	-24.0
Production	Pourers and casters, metal	51-4052	-2.0	-23.4
Office and administrative support	Computer operators	43-9011	-11.8	-22.8
Office and administrative support	Telephone operators	43-2021	-2.0	-22.6
Transportation and material moving	Mine shuttle car operators	53-7111	-0.3	-21.9
Production	Electromechanical equipment assem	51-2023	-9.8	-21.4
Office and administrative support	Data entry keyers	43-9021	-43.3	-21.2
Management occupations	Postmasters and mail superintendent	11-9131	-3.0	-20.9
Production	Electrical and electronic equipment a	51-2022	-45.6	-20.8
Production	Coil winders, tapers, and finishers	51-2021	-2.9	-20.7
Production	Grinding and polishing workers, hand	51-9022	-5.4	-20.5
Production	Timing device assemblers and adjust	51-2093	-0.2	-20.1
Office and administrative support	Switchboard operators, including ans	43-2011	-18.5	-19.9
Production	Prepress technicians and workers	51-5111	-6.9	-19.9
Production	Drilling and boring machine tool sette	51-4032	-2.4	-19.5
Production	Textile knitting and weaving machine	51-6063	-4.3	-19.3
Production	Milling and planing machine setters,	51-4035	-3.4	-19.3
Production	Forging machine setters, operators,	51-4022	-3.7	-19.2
Office and administrative support	Legal secretaries	43-6012	-37.1	-19.1
Production	Photographic process workers and p	51-9151	-4.9	-18.1
Production	Textile bleaching and dyeing machin	51-6061	-2.0	-18.1
Production	Aircraft structure, surfaces, rigging, a	51-2011	-7.3	-17.4
Office and administrative support	Executive secretaries and executive a	43-6011	-119.2	-17.4
Production	Engine and other machine assemble	51-2031	-6.5	-17.2

Fig. 9 Fastest growing and declining occupations in the BLS Employment Projections, 2016–2026

Category activities	Activity	Level 1	Level 2	Level 3
Information Input	Estimating the Quantifiable Characteristics of Products, Events, or Information	Estimate the size of household furnishings to be crated	Estimate the time required to evacuate a city in the event of a major	Estimate the amount of natural resources that lie beneath the world's
	Getting Information	Follow a standard blueprint	Review a budget	Study international tax laws
	Identifying Objects, Actions, and Events	Test an automobile transmission	Judge the acceptability of food products	Determine the reaction of a virus to a new drug
	Inspecting Equipment, Structures, or Material	Check that doors to building are locked	Inspect equipment in a chemical processing plant	Inspect a nuclear reactor
	Monitor Processes, Materials, or Sorroundings	Check to see if baking bread is done	Test electrical circuits	Check the status of a patient in critical medical care
Mental Processes	Analyzing Data or Information	Determine the location of a lost order	Determine the interest cost to finance a new building	Analyze the cost of medical care services for all hospitals in the country
	Developing Objectives and Strategies	Plan the holiday schedule for an airline workforce	Develop the plan to complete the merger of two organizations over a 3-	Develop a 10-year business plan for an organization
	Evaluating Information to Determine Compliance with Standards	Review forms for completeness	Evaluate a complicated insurance claim for compliance with policy	Make a ruling in court on a complicated motion
	Judging the Qualities of Things, Services, or People	Determine whether to remove a tree that has been damaged	Determine the value of property lost in a fire	Establish the value of a recently discovered ancient art work
	Making Decisions and Solving Problems	Determine the meal selection for a cafeteria	Select the location for a major department store	Make the final decision about a company's 5-year plan
	Organizing, Planning, and Prioritizing Work	Organize a work schedule that is repetitive and easy to plan	Plan and organize your own activities that often change	Prioritize and plan multiple tasks several months ahead
	Processing Information	Tabulate the costs of parcel deliveries	Calculate the adjustments for insurance claims	Compile data for a complex scientific report
	Scheduling Work and Activities	Make appointments for patients using a predetermined schedule	Prepare the work schedule for salesclerks in a large retail store	Schedule a complex conference program with multiple, parallel
	Thinking Creatively	Change the spacing on a printed report	Adapt popular music for a high school marching band	Create new computer software
	Updating and Using Relevant Knowledge	Keep up with price changes in a small retail store	Keep current on changes in maintenance procedures for repairing	Learn information related to a complex and rapidly changing
Work Output	Controlling Machines and Processes	Operate a cash register	Operate a drilling rig	Operate a precision milling machine
	Documenting/Recording Information	Record the weights of trucks that use the highways	Document the results of a crime scene investigation	Maintain information about the use of orbiting satellites for private industry
	Drafting, Laying Out, and Specifying Technical Devices, Parts, and Equipment	Specify the lighting for a work area	Specify the furnishings for a new school	Draw the electronic circuitry for a high-speed scientific computer
	Handling and Moving Objects	Change settings on copy machines	Arrange books in a library	Load boxes on an assembly line
	Interacting with Computers	Enter employee information into a computer database	Write software for keeping track of parts in inventory	Set up a new computer system for a large multinational company
	Operating Vehicles, Mechanized Devices, or Eqiuipment	Drive a car	Drive an 18-wheel tractor-trailer	Hover a helicopter in strong wind
	Performing General Physical Activities	Walk between work stations in a small office	Paint the outside of a house	Climb up and down poles to install electricity
	Repairing and Maintaining Electronic Equipment	Use knobs to adjust a television picture	Make repairs by removing and replacing circuit boards	Use complex test equipment to calibrate electronic equipment
	Repairing and Maintaining Mechanical Equipment	Make simple, external adjustments to a door hinge with ordinary hand tools	Adjust a grandfather clock	Overhaul a power plant turbine
Interacting with Others	Assisting and Caring for Others	Help a coworker complete an assignment	Assist a stranded traveler in finding lodging	Care for seriously injured persons in an emergency room
	Coaching and Developing others	Show a coworker how to operate a piece of equipment	Provide on-the-job training for clerical workers	Coach a college athletic team
	Communicating with Persons Outside Organization	Have little contact with people outside the organization	Make standard presentations about available services	Prepare or deliver press releases
	Communicating with Supervisors, Peers, or Subordinates	Write brief notes to others	Report the results of a sales meeting to a supervisor	Create a videotaped presentation of a company's internal policies
	Coordinating the Work and Activities of Others	Exchange information during a shift change	Organize the cleanup crew after a major sporting event	Act as general contractor for building a large industrial complex
	Developing and Building Teams	Encourage two coworkers to stick with a tough assignment	Lead an assembly team in an automobile plant	Lead a large team to design and build a new aircraft
	Establishing and Maintaining Interpersonal Relationsships	Exchange greetings with a coworker	Maintain good working relationships with almost all coworkers and clients	Gain cooperation from a culturally diverse group of executives hostile to
	Guiding, Directing, and Motivating Subordinates	Work occasionally as a backup supervisor	Supervise a small number of subordinates in a well-paid industry	Manage a severely downsized unit
	Interpreting the Meaning of Information for other	Interpret a blood pressure reading	Interpret how foreign tax laws apply to U.S. exports	Interpret a complex experiment in physics for general audiences
	Monitoring and Controlling Resources	Work as a housekeeper responsible for keeping track of linens	Work as a chef responsible for ordering food for the menu	Serve as a financial executive in charge of a large company's budget
	Performing Administrative Activities	Complete routine paperwork on standard forms	Complete tax forms required of self-employed people	Serve as the benefits director for a large computer sales organization
	Performing for or Wokring Directly with the public	Tend a highway toll booth	Sell shoes in a popular shoe store	Perform a monologue on national TV
	Provide Consultation and Advice to Others	Work in a position that requires little advising of others	Recommend a new software package to increase operational efficiency	Provide ideas for changing an organization to increase profitability
	Resolving Conflicts and Negotiation with Others	Apologize to a customer who complains about waiting too long	Get two subordinates to agree about vacation schedules	Negotiate a major labor-management contract
	Selling or Influencing Others	Convince a coworker to assist with an assignment	Deliver standard arguments or sales pitches to convince others to buy	Deliver major sales campaign in a new market
	Staffing Organizational Units	Work in a position that has minimal staffing requirements	Interview candidates for a sales position and make hiring	Direct a large recruiting and employment program for a large
	Training and Teaching Others	Give coworkers brief instructions on a simple procedural change	Teach a social sciences course to high school students	Develop and conduct training programs for a medical school

Fig. 10 Work activities and scores for automatability for different levels of complexity of tasks

	'Making' sectors (Producing & developing, Supplying & supporting)	Applying sectors	Complementary (Inhibiting & facilitating)	Spillover (E.g. quaternary)
Existing occupations	+ Engineers Robot designer; Robotic system engineer; Robotic system designer; Software engineers; Electrical & electronics engineers	- Examiners, investigators, readers, data keyers Buyers and purchasing agents; Claims adjusters, appraisers, examiners, and investigators; Insurance underwriters; Survey researchers; Parking enforcement workers; Communications equipment operators; Bill and account collectors; Dispatchers, except emergency; Meter readers, utilities; Computer operators; Parking lot attendants; Data entry keyers; Desktop publishers; - Assemblers, laborers & farm workers Electrical, electronics, and electromechanical assemblers; Aircraft structure, surfaces, rigging, and systems assemblers; Engine and other machine assemblers; Farmworkers and laborers, crop, nursery, and greenhouse; Inspectors, testers, sorters, samplers, and weighers; Graders and sorters; Forest Conversation Workers; Miscellaneous assemblers and fabricators; - Transportation & material movers Locomotive firers; Material moving workers; Hoist and winch operators; Industrial truck and tractor operators; - Clerks, accountants and secretaries Bookkeeping, accounting, and auditing clerks; Payroll and timekeeping clerks; Procurement Clerks; Correspondence Clerks, Order Clerks; Mail Clerks and mail machines operators; Office clerks; Executive secretaries; Legal secretaries; - Machine/ equipment setters, operators, tenders Forming machine setters, operators, and tenders; Machine tool cutting setters, operators, and tenders; Metal furnace operators, tenders, pourers, and casters; Chemical plant and system operator; Camera operators, television, video, and motion picture; - Model, die and pattern makers Molders and molding machine setters, operators, and tenders; Welding, soldering, and brazing workers; Miscellaneous metal and plastics workers; Structural metal fabricators and fitters; Tool and die makers; Prepress technicians and workers;	+/- Teachers, trainers, educators +/- Lawyers, legal secretary work +/- Incubators, business consultants	+/- Recreation, leisure +/- Sports, fitness, lifestyle Fitness Trainers and Instructors; Massage Therapists; Athletes; +/- Arts, culture, entertainment Musicians and singers; Producers and directors; Multimedia artists and animators; Actors; Art directors; Music directors and composers; Craft artists; Dancers; +/- Traveling Flight attendants; Water transportation workers; Lodging Managers; Airline & commercial pilots; +/- Health & personal care services
Exploiting & transforming occupations		+/- Machine programmers, production system designers, installation & maintenance engineers, industrial engineers Computer numerically controlled machine tool programmers, metal and plastic Industrial engineers, including health and safety; Mechanical Engineers; Industrial machinery installation, repair, and maintenance workers; +/- Information and data handlers & collectors Mathematicians; Statisticians; Operations research analyst Stock clerks and order fillers; Human resource specialists; Customer service representative; First-line supervisors of transportation and material-moving; Receptionists and information clerks		
Emerging occupations	+ Robotics & software engineer in health care, agriculture, construction, education Bioinformatician; Ergonomic designer Medical Equipment designer; Agricultural Informatics and Engineering Expert; + Big data and information system engineers Big data model designer; Information Systems architects;; Composite Engineer; Smart Management Systems Architect;	+ Big data analysist model & system: Telemetric data interpretation engineer; Operating Data Analyst; + Operators of systems in health care, agriculture, information systems, construction, security, education, etc. Medical Data Manager; Medical Robot Operator Remote Security Coordinator; Automated farming equipment operator; Robot attendant 3D printing designer in construction; Smart Travel System Designer; Clothes 3D model programmer;	+ Education, legal work, consulting in new technology (e.g. robot handling trainer, robotics lawyer, consultant specialized in application of robots, big data, or AI)	+ New media and art experiences Media Software Designer; Game designer Virtual & augmented reality engineer

Fig. 11 Technology-affected occupations classified according to sector and type of change of the occupation

References

Acemoglu, D.; Restrepo, P. *Robots and Jobs: Evidence from US Labor Markets*; NBER Working Paper; Social Science Electronic Publishing, Inc.: Rochester, NY, USA, 2017.

Acemoglu, D.; Restrepo, P. *Artificial Intelligence, Automation and Work*; NBER Working Paper; Social Science Electronic Publishing, Inc.: Rochester, NY, USA, 2018.

Arntz, M.; Gregory, T.; Zierahn U. *The Risk of Automation for Jobs in OECD Countries: A Comparative Analysis*; OECD Social, Employment and Migration Working Papers; OECD Publishing: Paris, France, 2016.

Arntz, M.; Gregory, T.; Zierahn, U. Revisiting the Risk of Automation. *Econ. Lett.* **2017**, *159*, 157–160.

Autor, D.H. Why are there still so many jobs? The history and future of workplace automation. *J. Econ. Perspect.* **2015**, *29*, 3–30.

Autor, D.H.; Katz, L.F.; Kearney, M.S. *The Polarization of the US Labor Market*; NBER Working Paper; Social Science Electronic Publishing, Inc.: Rochester, NY, USA, 2006.

Autor, D.H.; Levy, F.; Murnane, R.J. The Skill Content of Recent Technological Change: An Empirical Exploration. *Q. J. Econ.* **2003**, *118*, 1279–1333.

Autor, D.H; Salomons, A.M. Is automation labor-displacing? Productivity growth, employment, and the labor share. In Proceedings of the BPEA Conference Drafts, Detroit, MI, USA, 8–9 March 2018.

Autor, D. *Polanyi's Paradox and the Shape of Employment Growth*; NBER Working Paper; Social Science Electronic Publishing, Inc.: Rochester, NY, USA, 2014.

Basu, S.; Fernald, J.G.; Kimball, M.S. Are technology improvements contractionary? *Am. Econ. Rev.* **2006**, *96*, b1418–1448.

Baumol, W.J. Macroeconomics of Unbalanced Growth: The Anatomy of Urban Crisis. *Am. Econ. Rev.* **1967**, *57*, 415–426.

Bonin, H.; Gregory, T.; Zierahn, U. Übertragung der Studie von Frey/Osborne (2013) auf Deutschland. *ZEW Kurzexpertise* **2015**, *57*.

Bresnahan, T.F.; Trajtenberg, M. General purpose technologies: "Engines of growth". *J. Econom.* **1995**, *65*, 83–108.

Brynjolfsson, E.; McAfee, A. *Race Against the Machine: How the Digital Revolution is Accelerating Innovation, Driving Productivity, and Irreversibly Transforming Employment and the Economy*; Digital Frontier Press: Lexington, MA, USA, 2011.

Brzeski, C.; Burk, I. Die Roboter kommen. Folgen der Automatisierung für den deutschen Arbeitsmarkt. *INGDiBa Econ. Res.* **2015**, *30*, 1–7.

Colombino, U. Is unconditional basic income a viable alternative to other social welfare measures? *IZA World Labor* **2015**, *128*.

Dauth, W.; Findeisen, S.; Südekum, J.; Wößner, N. *German Robots—The Impact of Industrial Robots on Workers*; IAB: New York, NY, USA, 2017.

Deming, D.J. *The Growing Importance of Social Skills in the Labor Market*; NBER Working Paper; Social Science Electronic Publishing, Inc.: Rochester, NY, USA, 2015.

Dobbs, R.; Madgavkar, A.; Barton, D.; Labaye, E.; Manyika, J.; Roxburgh, C.; Lund, S.; Madhav, S. *The World at Work: Jobs, Pay, and Skills for 3.5 Billion People*; McKinsey Global Institute: Washington, DC, USA, 2012.

Echevarria, C. Changes in sectoral composition associated with economic growth. *Int. Econ. Rev.* **1997**, *38*, 431–452.

European Commission. *Towards Common Principles of Flexicurity. More and Better Jobs through Flexibility and Security*; Luxembourg Office for Official Publications of the European Communities: Liebefeld, Switzerland, 2007.

Forge, S.; Blackman, C. A Helping Hand for Europe: The Competitive Outlook for the EU Robotics Industry. In *Institute for Prospective Technological Studies*; JRC Scientific and Technical Report: EUR 24600 EN; Joint Research Centre, European Commission: Brussels, Belgium, 2010.

Ford, M. *The Rise of the Robots: Technology and the Threat of Mass Unemployment*; Oneworld Publications: Oxford, UK, 2015.

Frey, C.B.; Osborne, M.; Holmes, C.; Rahbari, E.; Garlick, R.; Friedlander, G.; McDonald, G. *Technology at Work v2. 0: The Future is not What it Used to Be*; CityGroup and University of Oxford: Oxford, UK, 2016.

Frey, C.B.; Osborne, M. The future of employment: how susceptible are jobs to computerisation? *Technol. Forecast. Soc. Chang.* **2017**, *114*, 254–280.

Gasteiger, E.; Prettner, K. *A Note on Automation, Stagnation, and the Implications of a Robot Tax*; Discussion Paper; School of Business & Economics, Freie Universität Berlin: Berlin, Germany, 2017.

Goldin, C.; Katz, L.F. The Origins of Technology—Skill Complementarity. *Q. J. Econ.* **1998**, *113*, 693–732.

Goldin, C.; Katz, L.F. *The Race between Education and Technology: The Evolution of U.S. Educational Wage Differentials, 1890 to 2005*; NBER Working Paper; Social Science Electronic Publishing, Inc.: Rochester, NY, USA, 2007.

Goos, M.; Manning, A. Lousy and lovely jobs: The rising polarization of work in Britain. *Rev. Econ. Stat.* **2007**, *89*, 118–133.

Goos, M.; Manning, A.; Salomons, A. Job polarization in Europe. *Am. Econ. Rev.* **2009**, *99*, 58–63.

Gorle, P.; Clive, A. *Positive Impact of Industrial Robots on Employment*; IFR: Frankfurt, Germany, 2013.

Graetz, G.; Michaels, G. *Robots at Work*; CEP Discussion Papers; Centre for Economic Performance, London School of Economics and Political Science: London, UK, 2015.

Gregory, T.; Salomons, A.; Zierahn, U. *Racing With or Against the Machine? Evidence from Europe*; Discussion Paper No. 16-053; ZEW: Mannheim, Germany, 2016.

Griliches, Z. Capital—Skill Complementarity. *Rev. Econ. Stat.* **1969**, *51*, 465–468.

Helpman, E.; Trajtenberg, M. Diffusion of General Purpose Technologies. In *General Purpose Technologies and Economic Growth*; Helpman, E., Ed.; MIT Press: Cambridge, MA, USA, 1997.

Keynes, J.M. *A Treatise on Money: The Applied Theory of Money*; AMS Press: New York, NY, USA, 1930.

Katz, L.F.; Margo, R.A. *Technical Change and the Relative Demand for Skilled Labor: The United States in Historical Perspective*; NBER Working Paper; Social Science Electronic Publishing, Inc.: Rochester, NY, USA, 2013.

Leontief, W. Technological Advance, Economic Growth, and the Distribution of Income. *Popul. Dev. Rev.* **1983**, *9*, 403–410.

Levy, F.; Murnane, R.J. How Computerized Work and Globalization Shape Human Skill Demands. In *Learning in the Global Era: International Perspectives on Globalization and Education*; Suarez-Orozco, M., Ed.; University of California Press: Berkeley, CA, USA, 2007; pp. 158–174.

MacCrory, F.; Westerman, G.; Alhammadi, Y.; Brynjolfsson, E. Racing with and against the machine: Changes in occupational skill composition in an era of rapid technological advance. In Proceedings of the Thirty Fifth International Conference on Information Systems, Auckland, New Zealand, 14–17 December 2014.

Manyika, J.; Chui, M.; Bughin, J.; Dobbs, R.; Bisson, P.; Marrs, A. *Disruptive Technologies: Advances that will Transform Life, Business, and the Global Economy*; McKinsey Global Institute: San Francisco, CA, USA, 2013.

Manyika, J.; Chui, M.; Miremadi, M.; Bughin, J.; George, K.; Willmott, P.; Dewhurst, M. *A Future that Works: Automation, Employment, and Productivity*; McKinsey Global Institute: San Francisco, CA, USA, 2017.

Mokyr, J.; Vickers, C.; Ziebarth, N.L. The History of Technological Anxiety and the Future of Economic Growth: Is this Time Different? *J. Econ. Perspect.* **2015**, *29*, 31–50.

Moretti, E.; Thulin, P. Local multipliers and human capital in the United States and Sweden. *Ind. Corp. Chang.* **2013**, *22*, 339–362.

Ngai, L.R.; Pissarides, C.A. Structural Change in a Multisector Model of Growth. *Am. Econ. Rev.* **2007**, *97*, 429–443.

Pasinetti, L. *Structural Change and Economic Growth: A Theoretical Essay on the Dynamics of the Wealth of Nations*; Cambridge University Press: Cambridge, UK, 1981.

Parijs, P.v. *Real Freedom for All, What (If Anything) can Justify Capitalism*; Clarendon Press: Oxford, UK, 1995.

Rodrik, D. Premature Deindustrialization. *J. Econ. Growth* **2016**, *21*, 1–33.

Saviotti, P.P.; Pyka, A. Economic development, qualitative change and employment creation. *Struct. Chang. Econ. Dyn.* **2004**, *15*, 265–287.

Saviotti, P.P.; Pyka, A. Product variety, competition and economic growth. *J. Evol. Econ.* **2008**, *18*, 323–347.

Schumpeter, J.A. *Capitalism, Socialism and Democracy*; Harper & Row: New York, NY, USA, 1942.

Schwab, K. *The Fourth Industrial Revolution*; Penguin: London, UK, 2017.

Stewart, I.; De, D.; Cole, A. *Technology and People: The Great Job-Creating Machine*; Deloitte: London, UK, 2015.

Trehan, B. Productivity Shocks and the Unemployment Rate. *FRBSF Econ. Rev.* **2003**, 13–27.

Vivarelli, M. *Innovation and employment Technological Unemployment Is Not Inevitable—Some Innovation Creates Jobs, and Some Job Destruction Can Be Avoided*; IZA Technical Report; Forschungsinstitut zur Zukunft der Arbeit (IZA): Bonn, Germany, 2007.

Vivarelli, M. Innovation, employment, and skills in advanced and developing countries: A survey of the economic literature. *J. Econ. Issues* **2014**, *48*, 123–154.

Wolfgang, M. *The Robotics Market—Figures and Forecasts*; RoboBusiness, Boston Consulting Group: Boston, MA, USA, 2016.

Appendix B
SRISTI: A Case Study

Society for Research and Initiatives for Sustainable Technologies and Institutions (SRISTI) is an organization to help rural people and give them a platform to sell and market their products. It was established in 1993 and is a developmental voluntary organization aiming to strengthen the creativity for grassroots communities, and individual innovators. It supports eco-friendly solutions to local problems being scouted, spawned and spread by the Honey Bee Network for over 33 years. It also nurtures eco-preneurs engaged in conserving biodiversity, common property resources, cultural diversity and educational innovations. There are five pillars of Honey Bee Network which SRISTI is committed to reinforce:

- Educational innovations by school and college teachers, students and other stakeholders.
- Institutional innovations at community and other levels in managing resources.
- Improving access of knowledge-rich, economically poor people to trigger self-reliant development process.
- Cultural creativity so that curiosity, collaboration, and compassion grow through art, literature and crafts, etc.
- Technological innovations and traditional knowledge dealing with human, animal, plant and ecosystem health, and policy reforms to generate frugal innovations for sustainable development at all levels, with specific reference to youth, children, women and elderly.

SRISTI has helped establish GIAN (Gujarat Grassroots Innovation Augmentation Network), National Innovation Foundation (NIF), and Micro Venture Innovation Fund (MVIF), Techpedia.sristi.org and AASTIIK (Academy for Augmenting Sustainable Technological Inventions, Innovations and Traditional Knowledge) in support of innovators and their innovations. SRISTI created the Honey Bee database of innovations, and supports the publication of the Network's newsletter in many

N. Shah, *Artificial Intelligence and Social Ethics*,
https://doi.org/10.1007/978-981-96-8818-0

languages. These are: Honey Bee (English), Gujarati (Loksarvani), Hindi (Sujh-Bujh Aas Paas Ki), Tamil (Num Vazhi Velanmai), Telugu (Palle Srujana), Malayalam (Ini Karshakan Samsarikkatte), and Odia (Aama Akha Pakha). Over the years, it has worked on neglected domains like women's knowledge systems, value addition through Sadbhav-SRISTI-Sanshodhan, a natural product laboratory. SRISTI organizes Shodh Yatra (walking Journey of Exploration, https://www.sristi.org/shodhyatra/), Traditional Food Festival, Biodiversity, Idea and Recipe Competitions and maintains a repository of numerous grassroots innovations, traditional knowledge, engineering students' projects, educational, cultural, and institutional innovations.

SRISTI has been advocating for protecting knowledge rights of creative communities and individuals. It has organized several consultative sessions with the private sector, scientists, activists and development workers for discussing various issues related to the access to bio-diversity and associated knowledge rights. It has also organized worldwide contest for scouting and rewarding innovations at grassroots in collaboration with IFAD (The International Fund for Agricultural Development), Rome.

Techpedia.in, another initiative of SRISTI, aims at putting the problems of micro, small and medium enterprises, informal sector, grassroots innovators and other social sectors on the agenda of the young technology students across the country. The industry and academic institutions can collaborate, co-create and foster distributed innovations and promote both horizontal and vertical learning and sharing through this platform. SRISTI has also instituted three categories of national awards for innovative students/faculty projects in engineering, pharmacy, biotechnology, basic sciences and other applied technologies in the form of Gandhian Young Technological Innovation Award (GYTI) since 2012 to promote a culture of innovation among the young minds of the country. Recently, BIRAC (Biotechnology Industry Research Assistance Council) has joined hands to reward 15 most powerful ideas in biomedical technologies and also support students in 100 socially relevant technologies at the idea or prototype stage.

SRISTI Samman is given periodically to outstanding social change agents. SRISTI is trying to build an online sanctuary of social, technological and institutional innovations through blend of open innovation, collaborative design, crowd-funding, incubation, e-commerce and challenge awards. We invite volunteers and collaborators to join us in this initiative.

Philosophy of Eight Es

These provide a framework for societies seeped in mediocrity to get over their inertia and move towards a compassionate, creative, competitive as well as collaborative society.

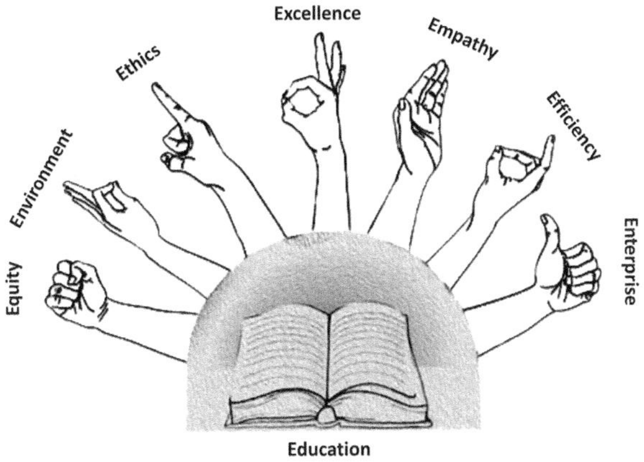

The ethical fulcrum of SRISTI can be captured by eight Es (ethics, empathy, equity, efficiency, excellence, environment, education and entrepreneurship)—the values that are central to the existence of Honey Bee Network.

Honey Bee Philosophy

Honey Bee signifies a philosophy of discourses, which is fair, authentic and accountable. It advocates people-to-people learning. The ethics of knowledge extraction, its documentation, dissemination and their abstraction into theories or technologies is the central concern of the Honey Bee Network. Despite all claims about participatory research and action, seldom have we provided opportunity to creative innovators and traditional knowledge holders to do research themselves as well as in partnership or by hiring formal researchers. The institutional scientists have often only spoken about the cause of collegial partnership with the local communities and people without taking proper steps for intellectual participation of communities. An evidence of this problem is that almost no research council in developed or developing country requires local knowledge providers in villages to be acknowledged by their name and address. Most institutions do not insist on their prior informed consent. Although the scenario is changing in some of the developed countries, the lack of accountability towards knowledge providers is still inadequate in developing countries. The principles we can learn from the life of honeybee are: Just as flowers do not complain when their nectar or pollen are taken away, people should not complain when their knowledge is documented by outsiders. But the knowledge providers should be acknowledged by their name and address and their intellectual property rights should be respected.

The bees perform a very important function of cross-pollination thereby enriching diversity and ensuring the continuity of Nature's cycle. Unless we communicate in vernaculars in a manner that people can understand, people-to-people linkages will not be established and horizontal learning will not take place. Whenever any wealth is generated by disseminating people's knowledge through commercial or non-commercial channel after adding value or without it, a fair share should go back to the people whose knowledge made that wealth possible.

Before disseminating people's knowledge or bringing it in public domain, their prior informed consent should be taken.

Honey Bee encourages collaborators to initiate local language versions of Honey Bee Newsletter, so that people-to-people learning across the barriers of language, culture and region can be facilitated. Honey Bee Network is a Knowledge Centre/Network which pools the solutions developed by people across the world in different sectors and links, not just the people, but also the formal and informal scientists, policy makers, innovators, green entrepreneurs and educationists and makes them available to others after taking relevant consent and due diligence.

The Honey Bee Network tries to: Provide a peer group of farmers, artisans, scientists, academics across language, culture and regional boundaries to nurture, critique and encourage innovative experimentation.

Break the nexus between the regions of high biodiversity and high poverty endowed with poor public as well as private infrastructure.

Provide access to information that can help improve productivity without increasing cost using other farmers' innovations. Most of the grassroots innovators do not have access to relevant information, which cripples their ability to raise resources and explore opportunities in different markets. Thus, poor demand for ecological and technological skills as well as their eco-friendly products forces them to become 'unskilled labourer' in the urban houses and markets.

Galvanize existing institutions and community structures to inspire and sustain the curiosity and spirit of younger generation to pursue the path of experimentation and excellence in local eco-enterprises and natural resource management.

Resolve an ethical dilemma about sharing and protecting traditional as well as contemporary knowledge of individuals and communities evolved through conscious efforts but guided by different value systems without keeping people poor. The fact that we have not found many young healers indicates that younger generation does not find the career of healer or herbalist worth pursuing when it entails a life of penury though with a lot of goodwill in the community.

Generate a system for rewarding and providing incentives to the innovative individuals as well communities under the provision of several international and national agreements like Convention on Biological Diversity (Art 8(J)), International Convention to Combat Desertification (Art 16), etc.

Success of SRISTI

SRISTI has succeeded on various fronts in addressing many challenges described above. We acknowledge the support provided by various agencies like SDC (Swiss Development Cooperation) (1981–1990), IDRC (International Development

Research Center) Canada, Pew Conservation Scholar Programme (award to Professor Gupta), Swedish Society for Nature and Conservation, MacArthur Foundation, University of Gothenburg, The Food and Agriculture Organization/Forests, Tree and People (FAO/FTP) Programme and Global Environment Facility (GEF), UNDP (The United Nations Development Programme), NISSAT (The National Information System for Science & Technology), UNICEF (United Nations Children's Fund), BIRAC, our innovators, collaborators and volunteers. However, we strongly feel that the real indicator of success will be when these activities can be sustained on their own through collective efforts of local innovators, investors and entrepreneurs in the near future. We are very much conscious of the need to transform these activities from the 'project mode' to a 'self-sustained polycentric Gandhian movement'.

Glossary

Artificial Intelligence: There are a number of definitions of Artificial Intelligence (AI). But John McCarthy, father of AI, offers the following definition in this 2004 paper, 'It is the science and engineering of making intelligent machines, especially intelligent computer programs. It is related to the similar task of using computers to understand human intelligence, but AI does not have to confine itself to methods that are biologically observable'.

Artificial Neural Networks (ANN): An Artificial Neural Network defines a mathematical model for the simulation of a network of biological neurons (e.g. human nervous system). It simulates different aspects related to the behaviour and capacity of the human brain, such as: intelligent information processing; distributed processing; high level of parallelism; faculty of learning, generalization and adaptation; high tolerance to inaccurate (or wrong) information (https://www.igi-global.com/).

B2B (business to business): Business-to-business (B2B) simply means business-to-business, which is a business model that works on selling products and/or provides services to other companies.

B2C (business to consumer): The term business-to-consumer (B2C) is a model for selling products and services directly to a business and consumers who are the end-users of its products or services. Most companies that sell directly to consumers can be referred to as B2C companies.

Big Data: The term 'big data' refers to data that is so large, fast or complex that it is difficult or impossible to process using traditional methods. The definition of big data is data that contains greater variety, arriving in increasing volumes and with more velocity. Hence, it is measure with three Vs: Volume, Velocity and Variety.

N. Shah, *Artificial Intelligence and Social Ethics*,
https://doi.org/10.1007/978-981-96-8818-0

Blind Spot Monitoring System (BSMS): Blind Spot Monitoring System is vehicle-based sensor system that detects other vehicles located to the driver's side and rear and send warnings to the driver. They may also include 'Rear Cross-Traffic Alert', which alerts driver about backing out of a parking space when traffic is approaching from the sides.

Blockchain: A blockchain is a decentralized ledger of all transactions across a peer-to-peer network. Using this technology, participants can confirm transactions without a need for a central clearing authority. Potential applications can include fund transfers, settling trades, voting, and many other issues (https://www.pwc.com/gx/en.html).

Building Automation System (BAS): A Building Automation System (BAS) is an intelligent system similar to SCADA, here both hardware and software, connecting heating, venting and air conditioning system, lighting, security, and other systems monitor and control on a single platform. This way the automation system is delivering you crucial information on the operational performance of a building as well as enhancing the safety and comfort of the occupants.

Chatbot: A chatbot is a computer programme that simulates and processes human conversation (either written or spoken), allowing humans to interact with digital devices as if they were communicating with a real person. Chatbots is a programme that answers a simple query with a single-line response, or as sophisticated as digital assistants that learn and evolve to deliver increasing levels of personalization as they gather and process information.

Cloud Computing Cloud Computing is on-demand access through the Internet, to computing resources, servers (physical servers and virtual servers), data storage, development tools, networking capabilities, and more—hosted at a remote data centre (Where voluminous data and applications have been stored) managed by a Cloud services provider (CSP). The CSP makes these resources available for a monthly subscription fee or bills them according to usage.

Cognitive Cloud Computing: Cognitive Cloud Computing is a kind of Cloud Computing which works on Deep Learning (DL) algorithms and Big Data analytics to provide insights of data.

Crowdsourcing: Crowdsourcing is obtaining work, information, or opinions from a large group of people who submit their data via the Internet, social media, and smartphone apps or other such platforms. Nowadays, many movements handle in a form of crowdsourcing.

Deep Learning: Deep Learning is a subset of Machine Learning. It also imitates the way human learn. It can be considered as automate predictive analysis where algorithms are complex and work in layers interconnected to each other. This interconnected network of algorithm is also known as Artificial Neural Network (ANN).

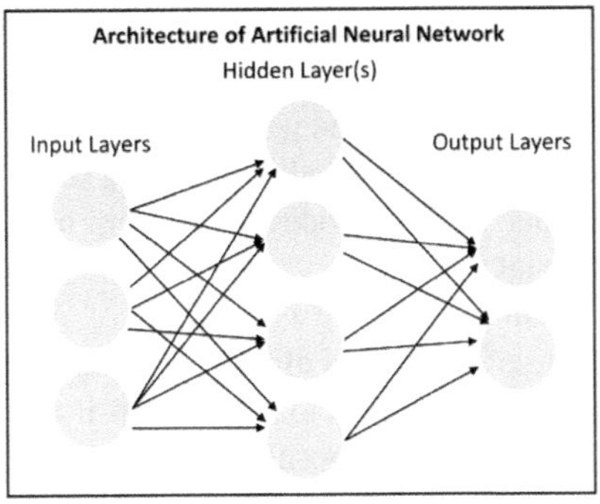

It is a hierarchical learning system with very large data where output of one layer become input of other layer.

E-mail Phishing: Phishing is a type of online scam where criminals impersonate legitimate organizations via e-mail, text message, advertisement or other means in order to steal sensitive information. This is usually done by including a link that will appear to take you to the company's website to fill in your information—but the website is a clever fake and the information you provide goes straight to the crooks behind the scam. When a link is provided through e-mail, it is called e-mail phishing.

Global Positioning System (GPS): The Global Positioning System (GPS) is a space-based radio-navigation system consisting of a constellation of satellites broadcasting navigation signals and a network of ground stations and satellite control stations used for monitoring and control (www.faa.gov). Since this is our existence in three dimensions, two or more satellites are used to collect data for a location.

Intelligent Agent: Intelligent agent is a computer programme that learn from the environment through sensor or input data and acting upon it through actuators. For example, Robot is an intelligent agent, it has camera, sensors, mechanical motors, etc. to sense the environment and actions are taken based on the input data like to move, to hold, to speak, etc.

Intelligent Parking Assist System (IPAS): Intelligent Parking Assist System is used to park vehicles in the parking area without intervention of humans. It takes the input from camera of different angles and sensors to identify path and obstacles. The system then takes over the steering control to maneuverer the vehicle.

Intelligent Tutoring System (ITS): Intelligent Tutoring System is a computer system that aims to provide immediate and customized instruction or feedback to learners through learning from the input of the learners. Here, learner does not require human intervention like a teacher. It is based on AI. It is beneficial for one-to-one interaction with learners.

IoT (Internet of Things): The Internet of Things is the concept of connecting any device (so long as it has an on/off switch) to the Internet and to other connected devices. The IoT is a giant network of connected things and people—all of which collect and share data about the way they are used and about the environment around them. The Internet of Things (IoT) describes the network of physical objects—'things'—that are embedded with sensors, software, and other technologies for the purpose of connecting and exchanging data with other devices and systems over the Internet. These devices range from ordinary household objects to sophisticated industrial tools.

Machine Learning: Machine Learning is a subset of Artificial Intelligence (AI) which focuses on the use of data and algorithms to imitate the way that humans learn, gradually allows the machine to learn from it and improve its accuracy. Machine Learning Glossary 207 algorithms work on sample data and train the model. Further, it uses the trained model to make decision or prediction for the new data of similar kind. ML can be divided into two types; supervised learning and unsupervised learning. Supervised learning is used when attributes are labelled and output is predefined. Unsupervised learning is used when attributes are not labelled or unknown.

Massive Open Online Course (MOOC): MOOC is online courses available for anyone to enrol. MOOCs provide an affordable and flexible way to learn new skills, advance your career and deliver quality educational experiences at scale. MOOCs are a widely researched development in distance education.

Natural Language Processing (NLP): Natural Language Processing is an automatic manipulation of language using computer programme for text, audio and images. It is always combined with linguistics. It is used with ML and DL. Speech operated GPS, speech to text or text to speech, translation in different language using computer programmes are examples of NLP

Over-the-Top (OTT): The acronym OTT means Over-the-Top, streaming across different devices whenever we want is possible because of 'over-the-top'. This is the latest delivery method of film and TV content over the Internet without the need for traditional broadcast, cable or satellite pay-TV providers

Quantum Computing: The quantum in 'quantum computing' refers to the quantum mechanics that the system uses to calculate outputs. In physics, a quantum is the smallest possible discrete unit of any physical property. It usually refers to properties of atomic or subatomic particles, such as electrons, neutrinos and photons

Supervisory Control and Data Acquisition (SCADA): Supervisory Control and Data Acquisition (SCADA) comprises software and hardware for the industrial organization. It collects and processes real time data that includes: monitor and control centralized system, control sensors, devices and data locally as well as remotely

Unmanned Aerial Vehicle (UAV): Unmanned Aerial Vehicle (UAV) is basically used for military tasks. Military aircraft that is guided autonomously, by remote control, or both and that carries 208 Glossary sensors, target designators, offensive ordnance, or electronic transmitters designed to interfere with or destroy enemy targets. Most of such devices are developed using AI and many other technologies.

Unmanned Ground Vehicle (UGV): Unmanned Ground Vehicle (UGV) is similar to UAV; unlike UAV it is operated while in contact with the ground and without an on-board human presence. UGVs can be used for many applications where it may be inconvenient, dangerous, or impossible to have a human operator present. Generally, the vehicle will have a set of sensors to observe the environment, and will make decisions about its behaviour or pass the information to a human operator at a different location who will control the vehicle. This is also supported by AI.

Video on Demand (VoD): Video on demand (VOD) is a media distribution system that allows users to access videos without the constraints of a typical static broadcasting schedule on the Internet platform. As Internet continued to develop in the 1990s, consumers began to gravitate towards non-traditional modes of content consumption, which culminated in the arrival of VOD on televisions and personal computers.

Virtual Reality (VR): Virtual reality (VR), the use of computer modelling and simulation that enables a person to interact with an artificial three-dimensional (3-D) visual or other sensory environment. VR applications immerse the user in a computer-generated environment that simulates reality through the use of interactive devices, which send and receive information and are worn as goggles, headsets, gloves, or body suits (Britannica.com)

Voice Assistance (VA): A voice assistant is a digital assistant that uses voice recognition, language processing algorithms, and voice synthesis to listen to specific voice commands and return relevant information or perform specific functions as requested by the user.

Bibliography

Acemoglu Daron and Pascual Restrepo (2018). Artificial Intelligence,Automation and Work. NBER working paper series—24196. https://doi.org/10.3386/w24196. https://www.nber.org/papers/w24196

Acemoglu, Daron and Pascual Restrepo (2017). Robots and Jobs: Evidence from US Labour Market. *Journal of Political Economy*. Volume 128. Number (6). pp. 2188–2244.

Aho, B. and R. Duffield. (2020). Beyond Surveillance Capitalism: Privacy, Regulation and Big Data in Europe and China. *Econ. Soc.* 2020, 1–26.

Allen, Greg and Taniel Chan. (2017). Artificial Intelligence and National Security. Belfer Center Paper. Belfer Center for Science and International Affairs, Harvard Kennedy School.

Allhoff, Fritz and Adam Henschke (2018). The Internet of Things: Foundational Ethical Issues. *Internet of Things*. Volumes 1–2, September 2018, pp. 55–66. https://doi.org/10.1016/j.iot.2018.08.005

Anderson, Jonas (2014). *Representing Human-Automation Challenges: A Model Based Approach for Human Factors Engineering in Industrial Practice*. Sweden: Chalmers University of Technology.

Bainbridge, L. (1983). Ironies of Automation. Automatica, 19, 775–779. https://doi.org/10.1016/0005-1098(83)90046-8

Boulanin, Vincent, Lora Saalman, Petr Topychkanov, Fei Su and Moa Peldán Carlsson (2020). *Artificial Intelligence, Strategic Stability and Nuclear Risk*. SIPRI. https://www.sipri.org/sites/default/files/2020-06/artificial_intelligence_strategic_stability_and_nuclear_risk.pdf

Brown, Justine, Tom Gosling, Bhushan Sethi, Blair Sheppard, Carol Stubbings, John Sviokla, Jon Williams and Daria Zarubina (2018). Workforce of the Future: The Competing Forces Shaping 2030. https://www.pwc.com/gx/en/services/people-organisation/workforce-of-the-future/workforce-of-the-future-the-competing-forces-shaping-2030-pwc.pdf

Brundage, Miles et al. (2018). The Malicious Use of Artificial Intelligence: Forecasting, Prevention, and Mitigation. ArxiV id: 1802.07228. http://arxiv.org/abs/1802.07228

Chui, Michael, James Manyika and Mehdi Miremadi (2016). Where Machines could Replace Humans—and Where they can't (yet)—The Technical Potential for Automation differs Dramatically across Sectors and Activities. ISBN 00475394.

Cogressional Research Service (2019). Artificial Intelligence and National Security. https://crsreports.congress.gov/R45178.pdf

Collins, Jonathan (2016). ABI Research Deems Voice Control the New Breakout Star in Smart Home Technology. Voice Control Will Account for Close to One Third of Smart Home Device Revenues by 2021. https://www.abiresearch.com/press/abi-research-deemsvoice-control-new-breakout-star/

Cypher, James M. (2014). *The Process of Economic Development*. 4th Edition, London: Routledge Taylor & Francis Group.

N. Shah, *Artificial Intelligence and Social Ethics*,
https://doi.org/10.1007/978-981-96-8818-0

Dellot, Benedict and Fabian Wallace Stephens (2017). *The Age of Automation: Artificial Intelligence, Robotics and The Future of low skilled Work*. RSA Action and Research Center.

Dhaliwal, A., G.S. Sukhadme and A.A.G. Requicha (2004). Bacterium Inspired Robots for Environment Monitoring, IEEE International Conference on Robotics and Automation paper presented at the proceeding.

Erin, Winick (2018). Every Study we could find on What Automation will do to Jobs, in One Chart. https://www.technologyreview.com/2018/01/25/146020/every-study-we-could-find-on-what-automation-willdoto-jobs-in-one-chart/

Forbus, K.D. and J. Laird (2002). AI and the Entertainment Industry Intelligent Systems, IEEE 17(4):15–16. https://doi.org/10.1109/MIS.2002.1024746. Source IEEE Xplore.

Forti, V., C.P. Balde, R. Kuehr and G. Bel (2020). The Global E-waste Monitor 2020: Quantities, Flows and the Circular Economy Potential. United Nations University (UNU)/United Nations Institute for Training and Research (UNITAR)—co-hosted SCYCLE Programme, International Telecommunication Union (ITU) & International Solid Waste Association (ISWA), Bonn/Geneva/Rotterdam. ISBN Digital: 978–92–808–9114–0. ISBN Print: 978-92-808-9115-7.

Frey, Thomas (2012). 2 Billion Jobs to Disappear by 2030. https://futuristspeaker.com/business-trends/2-billion-jobs-to-disappear-by-2030/

Furman, Jason and Robert Seamans (2018). AI and the Economy. National Bureau of Economic Research. http://www.nber.org/papers/w24689

Gandhi, M.K. (1945). Constructive Programme (Its Meaning and Place). pp. 20–21 https://www.mkgandhi.org/ebks/construct.pdf

Ganguli, B.N. (2006). *Gandhi's Social Philosophy: Perspective and Relevance*. Radha Publications (1 January 2006). Gartner, https://www.gartner.com/en/newsroom

Gonzales, Richard (November 2019). Feds Say Self-Driving Uber SUV Did Not Recognize Jaywalking Pedestrian in Fatal Crash. https://www.npr.org/2019/11/07/777438412/feds-say-self-driving-uber-suv-did-not-recognize-jaywalking-pedestrian-in-fatal

Halpern, S. (2018). Cambridge Analytica and the Perils of Psychographics. Available at: https://www.newyorker.com/news/news-desk/cambridge-analytica-and-the-perils-of-psychographics

Hamet, P. and J. Tremblay (2017). Artificial Intelligence in Medicine. *Metabolism: Clinical and Experimental*. Volume 69S. pp. S36–S40. https://doi.org/10.1016/j.metabol.2017.01.011 Corpus ID: 206916359.

Harari, Y. (2018). 21 Lessons for the 21st Century. Jonathan Cape. *Harijan*, 31 March 1946, p. 63. Chapter 5: Economic Equality. https://www.mkgandhi.org/trusteeship/chap05.htm

Hayden, Ernie, Michael Assante and Tim Conway (2014). An Abbreviated History of Automation and Industrial Controls Systems and Cybersecurity. A SANS Analyst Whitepaper.

IFRS Press Room (2021). The International Federation of Robotics: https://ifr.org/ifr-press-releases/news/ifr-robots-improve-manufacturing-success-&-create-jobs.

Jivani, Siddharth (2018). Mahatma Gandhi on Machinery. https://www.oil-refinery.com/mahatma-gandhi-on-machinery.

Jonas, Hans (1984). The Imperative of Responsibility: In Search of an Ethics for the Technological Age. Chicago: University of Chicago Press. https://doi.org/10.1177/016224398501000419.

Joshi, Divya (2002). *Gandhiji on Villages*. Gandhi Book Centre, Mumbai. www.mkgandhi.org.

Joshi, Vidyut (2021). *Gandhian Humanism in Praxis*. Jaipur: Rawat Publications.

Kasapoðlu, Can and Barýþ Kýrdemir (2019). Wars Of None: Artificial Intelligence And The Future Of Conflict. Center for Economics and Foreign Policy Studies. https://edam.org.tr/wp-content/uploads/2019/05/EDAM_Wars-of-None-Artificial-Intelligence-and-the-Future-of-Conflict.pdf.

Kelly, Christopher J., Alan Karthikesalingam, Mustafa Suleyman, Greg Corrado and Dominic King (2019). Key Challenges for Delivering Clinical Impact with Artificial Intelligence BMC Medicine (2019) 17:195. https://doi.org/10.1186/s12916-019-1426-2

Kogle, Nishikant and Shreekumar N. (2011). Gandhi's Criticism of Industrialization and Modernity: An Environment Perspective. In Siby K. Joseph and Bharat Mahodaya (eds), *Gandhi, Environment and Sustainable Future,* Wardha: Institute of Gandhi Studies, Wardha. https://www.mkgandhi.org/ebks/environment.pdf

Kulkarni, Sudheendra (2012). *Music of the Spinning Wheel: Mahatma Gandhi's Manifesto for the INTERNET AGE.* Bhopal: Manjul Publishing House Pvt. Ltd.

Lighthill, James (1973). Artificial Intelligence: A General Survey. Published as part of Science Research Council, Artificial Intelligence: A Paper Symposium, London: SRC. pp. 1–21.

Malhotra, Rajiv (2021). *Artificial Intelligence and the Future of Power.* New Delhi: Rupa Publications India.

Manes, S. (2000), 'Private Lives? Not Ours!' PC World 18(6): 312.

McCarthy, John. (2007). What is Artificial Intelligence? Stanford University Stanford, CA 94305. http://jmc.stanford.edu/articles/whatisai/whatisai.pdf

Metra Martech Report, 2013. Positive Impact of Industrial Robots on Employment: https://robohub.org/wp-content/uploads/2013/04/Metra_Martech_Study_on_robots_2013.pdf

Miah, Andy (2013). Ethics Issues Raised By Human Enhancement. *Values and Ethics for the 21st Century.* BBVA. pp 167–196.

Mishra, Premanand (2015). *Gandhian Humanism in the Twenty First Century,* Rajasthan: IASE Deemed University.

Mishra, R.K. (17 May 2014). Gandhi's View on Modern Industrialism. Your Article Library.https://www.yourarticlelibrary.com/essay/gandhis-view-on-modern-industrialism/40282.

Nature Research (2019). What 5G Means for our Health. https://www.nature.com/articles/d42473-019-00009-7

O'Sullivan, David (2009). Industrial Automation Course Notes. Universidade do Minho May 2009. www.owl.ie

Osoba, Osonde and William Welser (2017). An Intelligence in Our Image The Risks of Bias and Errors in Artificial Intelligence. Library of Congress Cataloging-in-Publication Data is available for this publication.

Pazzanese, Christina (2020). Ethical Concerns Mount as AI takes Bigger Decision-making Role in more Industries. https://news.harvard.edu/gazette/story/2020/10/ethical-concerns-mount-as-ai-takes-bigger-decision-making-role/

Perrault, Raymond, Yoav Shoham, Erik Brynjolfsson, Jack Clark, John Etchemendy, Barbara Grosz, Terah Lyons, James Manyika, Saurabh Mishra, and Juan Carlos Niebles. (December 2019). 'The AI Index 2019 Annual Report', AI Index Steering Committee, Human-Centered AI Institute, Stanford University, Stanford, CA

Prasad, Sambhu (2001). Towards an Understanding of Gandhi's Views on Science. *Economic and Political Weekly* 2001. *Review of Science Studies Sept.* pp. 3721–32. https://www.mkgandhi.org/articles/views_on_sci.htm

Rao, Anand S. (2016). Five Myths and Facts about Artificial Intelligence. *Predictive Analysis and Futurism.* Issue 14. https://www.soa.org/globalassets/assets/Library/Newsletters/Predictive-Analytics-and-Futurism/2016/december/paf-iss14-rao.pdf

Rao, Anand S. (2018). Artificial Intelligence in India—Hype or Reality Impact of Artificial Intelligence across Industries and User Groups. https://www.pwc.in/assets/pdfs/consulting/technology/data-and-analytics/artificial-intelligence-in-india-hype-or-reality/artificialintelligence-in-india-hype-or-reality.pdf

Rao, Anand S. and Gerard Verweij (2017). PwC. Sizing the prize: What's the Real Value of AI for your Business and how can you Capitalise? https://www.pwc.com/gx/en/issues/analytics/assets/pwc-ai-analysis-sizing-the-prize-report.pdf

Regulation of Crypto-currency Around the World (2018). The Law Library of Congress, Global Legal Research Center. law@loc.gov.http://www.law.gov

Rigano, Christopher (2019). Using Artificial Intelligence to Address Criminal Justice Needs. *NIJ Journal*, p. 280.

Russell, Stuart J. and Peter Norvig (2010). *Artificial Intelligence: A Modern Approach.* Upper Saddle River, N.J.: Prentice Hall.

Saudi, Abdesalam (January 2018). Driverless Cars might Follow the Rules of the Road, but what about the Language of Driving?. https://theconversation.com/driverless-cars-might-follow-the-rulesof-the-road-but-what-about-the-language-of-driving-88824

Schmitt, Markus, Artificial Intelligence in Medicine AI for Diagnostics, Drug Development, Treatment Personalization, and Gene Editing. https://www.datarevenue.com/en-blog/artificial-intelligence-inmedicine

Schultz, Robert A. (2013). *Ethics and the Internet: Values and Ethics for the 21st Century.* BBVA. pp. 217–252.

Schwartz, Alexandra (2018). The Impact of Emerging Technology on the Media and Entertainment Industry https://medium.com/ @alex.schwartz/the-impact-of-emerging-technology-on-the-mediaentertainment-industry-e2e20899374b

Shah, Neepa (2014). Data Warehouse Systems in the Environment of Cloud Computing: A Comparative Study of Elastic Cloud Computing and Organizational Systems. International Conference on 'Computing for Sustainable Global Development', 5–7 March 2014. ISSN 0973–7529; ISBN 978–93–80544–11–3

Shah, Neepa (2015). Big Data and Cloud Computing: Pitfalls and Advantages in Data Management. 2nd International Conference on 'Computing for Sustainable Global Development', 11–13 March 2015. ISSN 0973-7529; ISBN 978-93-80544-14-4

Shantharam, Shanthu (2016). The Satyagrahi Scientist. https://swarajyamag.com/magazine/the-satyagrahi-scientist

Shields, Justin (2018). Smart Machines and Smarter Policy: Foreign Investment Regulation, National Security, and Technology Transfer in the Age of Artificial Intelligence, 51 *J. Marshall L. Rev.*

Smith, Chris, Brian McGuire, Ting Huang, Gary Yang (December 2006). The History of Artificial Intelligence. History of Computing, CSEP 590A, University of Washington.

Spiegeleire, Stephan De, Matthijs Maas and Tim Sweijs (2017). Artificial Intelligence and the Future of Defense: Strategic Implications For Small- And Medium-Sized Force Providers. The Hague Centre For Strategic Studies (HCSS).

Stone, Peter, Rodney Brooks, Erik Brynjolfsson, Ryan Calo, Oren Etzioni, Greg Hager, Julia Hirschberg, Shivaram Kalyanakrishnan, Ece Kamar, Kevin Leyton-Brown, David C. Parkes, William Press, AnnaLee Saxenian, Julie Shah, Milind Tambe and Astro Teller (2016). Artificial Intelligence and Life in 2030. One Hundred Year Study on Artificial Intelligence: Report of the 2015–2016 Study Panel. https://ai100.stanford.edu/sites/g/files/sbiybj9861/f/ai100report10032016fnl_singles.pdf

Sullins, John (2021). Information Technology and Moral Values, *The Stanford Encyclopedia of Philosophy*, https://plato.stanford.edu/archives/spr2021/entries/it-moral-values. Spring 2021. Metaphysics Research Lab, Stanford University.

Sutton, Brian (2013). 'The Effects of Technology in Society and Education' Education and Human Development Master's Theses. 192. http://digitalcommons.brockport.edu/ehd_theses/192.pdf.

Turing, A.M. (1950). Computing Machinery and Intelligence. *Mind*, 59, 433–460. https://doi.org/10.1093/mind/LIX.236.433.

UNESCO (2019). Artificial Intelligence in Education: Challenges and Opportunities for Sustainable Development. Published by the United Nations Educational, Scientific and Cultural Organization. https://www.gcedclearinghouse.org/sites/default/files/resources/190175eng.pdf.

UNESCO (2021). Artificial Intelligence: Examples of Ethical Dilemmas. https://en.unesco.org/artificial-intelligence/ethics/cases.

Vermeulen, Ben, Jan Kesselhut, Andreas Pyka and Pier Paolo Saviotti (2018). The Impact of Automation on Employment: Just the Usual Structural Change? *Sustainability* 2018, 10, 1661; https://doi.org/10.3390/su10051166.

Wade, Andrew (February 2019). How Artificial Intelligence is Transforming the World. https://www.theengineer.co.uk/ai-medicaldiagnostics/.

Wang, Weiyu and Keng Siau (2019). Artificial Intelligence, Machine Learning, Automation, Robotics, Future of Work and Future of Humanity: A Review and Research Agenda. *Journal of Database Management*, 30(1): 61–79.

West, Darrell M. and John R. Allen. (2018). How Artificial Intelligence is Transforming the World. https://www.brookings.edu/research/how-artificial-intelligence-is-transforming-the-world/.

Wheeler, Katherine S. (2015). The Relationships Between Television Viewing Behaviors, Attachment, Loneliness, Depression, and Psychological Well-Being. Honors College Theses. 98. https://digitalcommons.georgiasouthern.edu/honors-theses/98.

Winston, Patrick H. (1992). *Artificial Intelligence* (3rd ed). pp. I-XXV, 1–737. Addison-Wesley.

World Economic Forum (WEF). 2016. The Future of Jobs Employment, Skills and Workforce Strategy for the Fourth Industrial Revolution http://www3.weforum.org/docs/WEF_FOJ_Executive_Summary_Jobs.pdf.

Index

N. Shah, *Artificial Intelligence and Social Ethics*,
https://doi.org/10.1007/978-981-96-8818-0

GPSR Compliance

The European Union's (EU) General Product Safety Regulation (GPSR) is a set of rules that requires consumer products to be safe and our obligations to ensure this.

If you have any concerns about our products, you can contact us on ProductSafety@springernature.com

In case Publisher is established outside the EU, the EU authorized representative is:

Springer Nature Customer Service Center GmbH
Europaplatz 3
69115 Heidelberg, Germany

Batch number: 10704307

Printed by Printforce, the Netherlands